Deal Making

The Secrets of Successful Negotiations

Deal Making

The Secrets of Successful Negotiations

Marc Helmold

IU International University of Applied Sciences, Berlin, Germany

World Scientific

NEW JERSEY · LONDON · SINGAPORE · BEIJING · SHANGHAI · TAIPEI · CHENNAI

Published by

World Scientific Publishing Europe Ltd.

57 Shelton Street, Covent Garden, London WC2H 9HE

Head office: 5 Toh Tuck Link, Singapore 596224

USA office: 27 Warren Street, Suite 401-402, Hackensack, NJ 07601

Library of Congress Control Number: 2024058217

British Library Cataloguing-in-Publication Data
A catalogue record for this book is available from the British Library.

DEAL MAKING
The Secrets of Successful Negotiations

ISBN 9781800617124 (hardcover)
ISBN 9781800615366 (paperback)
ISBN 9781800617131 (ebook for institutions)
ISBN 9781800617148 (ebook for individuals)

For any available supplementary material, please visit
https://www.worldscientific.com/worldscibooks/10.1142/Q0504#t=suppl

Desk Editors: Murali Appadurai/Gabriel Rawlinson/Shi Ying Koe

Typeset by Stallion Press
Email: enquiries@stallionpress.com

*This book is dedicated to my parents,
my wife Takako, and my daughters.*

Preface

Negotiations are a dialogue between two or more parties and the process of conflict resolution to resolve points of difference and gain an advantage for an individual or group to satisfy various interests. Conflict negotiation is the process of resolving a dispute or a conflict permanently by providing for each side's needs and adequately addressing their interests so that they are satisfied with the outcome.

In conflict negotiation, the parties involved aspire to agree on matters of mutual interest. This may lead to an agreement which is beneficial for all or only some of the parties.

This book provides a holistic and practical approach to conflict resolution, negotiations, and deal making. Through a valuable overview of concrete negotiation situations in industry and business, including a variety of examples and use cases of how professionals reach deal-making breakthroughs, the author discusses ways to achieve successful negotiation.

Each chapter offers practical, use friendly, and immediately applicable tips, including outlining how questioning techniques can work to influence and manipulate the negotiation opponent, and the introduction of Dr. Marc Helmold's A-6 negotiation concept, which provides the ideal framework for successful negotiations and deals.

About the Author

Marc Helmold is a full-time professor at IU International University of Applied Sciences in Berlin, Germany, and he conducts workshops on negotiation, lean management, and leadership through his own consultancy, MaHeLeanCon. He has more than 20 years of experience conducting negotiations in the railway, automotive and aviation industries.

Contents

List of Figures

List of Tables

Chapter 1

Negotiations and Deals

1.1 Negotiations: Definition and Scope

Negotiations play an important role in many life situations, professional fields, and business relations. Global megatrends, ongoing crises, and advancing globalisation show us how vulnerable supply chains and the associated business relationships can be. Therefore, the importance of negotiations and related skills in an international context is growing, making them central to many companies (Weiss, 2022). While in the past it was mostly salespeople and buyers who were trained in negotiation techniques, today we see that departments such as development, logistics, quality, and finance, which are directly or indirectly involved in the value creation process, actively conduct or participate in negotiations (Schranner, 2015). The key to successful negotiations lies in good preparation, diligent practice, and a genuine appreciation of others (Kraus, 2022). The term "negotiation" originally comes from the Latin roots *nec* (English: no, none) and *otium* (free time), meaning "no free time". In contrast to the nobility (the patricians), the citizens of Rome had no free time amidst their daily trade and labour. In the 17th century, the term was modified in the French language to mean "business transaction, agreement and resolution of a conflict" (Helmold *et al.*, 2022). Negotiations are a form of communication, usually conducted through conversation (verbal dialogue), about a controversial issue characterised by opposing needs, interests, and motives. Basically, negotiations aim to achieve a balance of interests by weighing up the positions and the intensity of the needs, ultimately resulting in an agreement. Every individual or business entity has clear interests, desires, motives, and needs that they seek to realise. O'Brien defines negotiation as the process of reaching an agreement on a specific issue by at least two parties. In this context, all parties aim to achieve a balance of interests and resolve the conflict by finding common ground (O'Brien, 2016). Acceding (giving) and demanding (taking) are two central points in successful negotiations. Negotiations only occur when all parties take the initiative to find a common solution. Figure 1.1 shows the six key characteristics of negotiations:

- At least two or more parties must be involved.
- The goal of the parties must be to reach an agreement.
- The parties must strive to resolve a conflict amicably.
- All parties must be willing to give and take.
- A desired balance of interests must be achieved.
- All parties must take the initiative to find a solution.

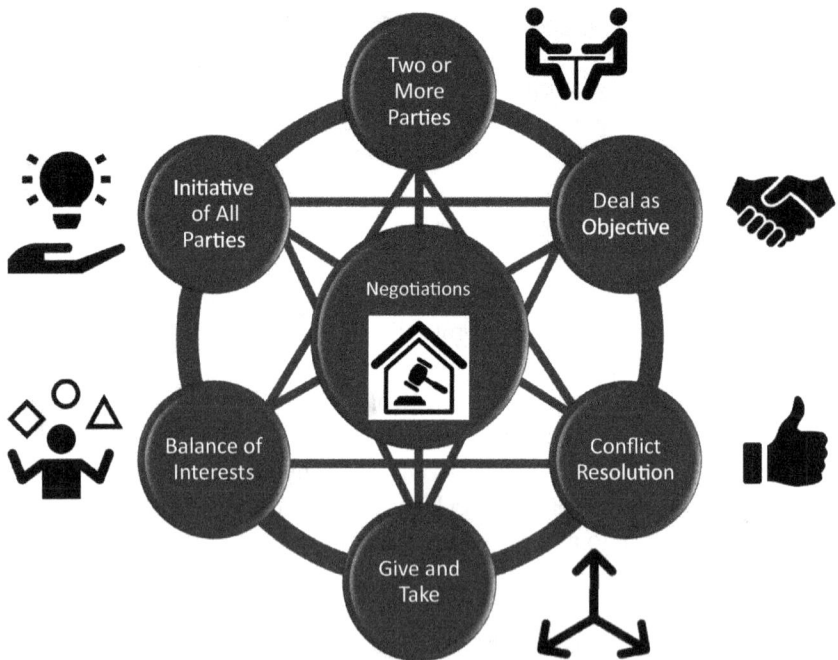

Figure 1.1.   Characteristics of negotiations.

The motives and needs in company negotiations can be of a different nature yet share the same characteristics. Buyers seek to achieve the lowest possible purchase price during transactions, whereas sellers strive for the highest possible sales price. Both sides aim for the optimal price for themselves. Internal company demands for a higher budget are also needs that must be addressed during internal company negotiations. For example, a company may require additional sales staff in order to expand into other countries and markets. Job interviews are also negotiations because they include the wishes and needs of the participants, namely to find the right employee or the right position. In addition to the actual job, there are numerous elements in job interviews, such as salary, fringe benefits, and social benefits, which are part of the negotiations. Not only in companies but also in private life, there are a multitude of needs that result in negotiations. For example, youngsters negotiate with their parents to fulfil their desire for electronic gadgets or clothing from certain brands. Similarly, you may negotiate with your family members regarding the destination of your next summer vacation.

All of these needs and desires represent negotiations concerning controversial issues and usually lead to a more or less consensual result. Negotiations involve interactions among two or more parties about a specific issue, where their fundamental interest is in reaching an agreement. These are characterised by an intended balance between the interests and the negotiated result. Experts agree that negotiations are diverse and occur in every conceivable area of life (Helmold *et al.*, 2022). The following are a few examples of negotiations in different life or business situations:

- price agreements for products and services between customer (buyer) and manufacturer (supplier);
- technical agreements on performance characteristics of products between customer and supplier;
- agreements between supplier and customer on the quality, performance, and specification characteristics of services;
- coalition negotiations between parties to form a government following elections;
- online auctions by the purchasing department of a large corporation for a major project;

- haggling with the seller at a flea market and the subsequent purchase of an antique piece of furniture;
- an oral final exam attended by students, where they answer questions posed by professors;
- negotiating a salary with the HR department during interviews;
- an employee requesting a salary increase from their supervisor, citing good performance;
- agreement on employee goals as part of the annual discussions between supervisor and employee;
- agreement between a freelance consultant and their client on project scope and workload;
- application process for honorary lecturers at a university to deliver lectures to economics students;
- discussion between parents and children about which restaurant to visit in the neighbourhood;
- children asking their parents for sweets when shopping in a supermarket;
- hostage situations, where the abductors make demands to the police, e.g., a getaway car.

1.2 Deal Making

A negotiation or deal is a strategic discussion between two parties to resolve an issue in a way that both find acceptable. Negotiations occur between buyers and sellers, employers and prospective employees, or the governments of two or more countries. Successful negotiations usually involve compromises on the part of one or all parties. Negotiations or Deals can be defined as the art of crafting agreements through negotiations that focus on an integrative, or value-creating, process rather than a distributive bargaining, or haggling, process.

The deal-making matrix, as shown in Figure 1.2, outlines the possibilities and outcomes of negotiations in relation to effort and time or duration. Low-effort or fast outcomes are ideal opportunities to give in and to ask for concessions. High-impact deals achievable with low effort or within short time durations should be prioritised as "quick deals". Low-effort or speedy activities with low-level outcomes or impacts are "time wasters", which should be avoided. "Big deal" outcomes over a longer time period should be well researched and analysed (Helmold, 2022).

Deal-Making Matrix Effort/Time

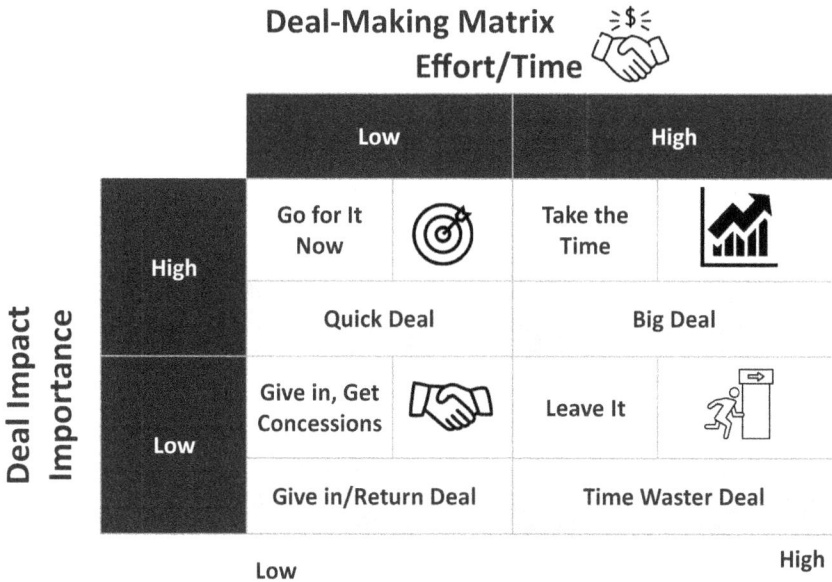

Figure 1.2. Deal-making matrix.

1.3 Success Factors in Negotiations

Negotiation is one of the core competencies of salespeople, buyers, and various other professional groups along the value chain of companies. Pressure often arises during sales negotiations when they are reduced to haggling over pricing. Such situations often lead to people having to agree to one-sided results against their will. Purchasing employees are often pushed to attain "cost savings" to achieve better margins. Project managers also negotiate with different stakeholders on a daily basis in a wide variety of situations with regard to quality, costs, or time. Every meeting with clients, report to management, or search for a solution with team members can be considered a form of negotiation. On the surface, negotiations often fail due to relationship problems, different perspectives, or steadfastness among the parties involved. On closer inspection, however, it becomes clear that conflicts of values, incompetence, or a lack of the understanding required for successful conclusion often act as obstacles during negotiations or cause them to fail entirely. In such deadlock situations, the A-6 negotiation framework proposed the author (2022) offers new options for action and a professional approach. Professionalism entails doing everything possible to achieve the best possible negotiation performance. This includes thorough preparation, the development of effective techniques, and continuous work on your own negotiating personality. Compared to previous models, such as the Harvard model, which focus on the factual and relationship aspects, the A-6 negotiation framework also takes personality traits and intercultural framework conditions into account. Thus, obstacles can be addressed in a targeted manner, and solutions of added value for all parties can be developed. Table 1.1 shows the most important factors for a successful negotiation breakthrough. Negotiations require effective time and process management, with a focus on efficiency. Negotiations should be relationship-based to foster an amicable atmosphere among participants. Balance and harmony are significant attributes for successful negotiations in this context. Negotiators must create mutual understanding and demonstrate communication skills. Communication skills include both willingness and ability to listen and effectively convey oral and written information in an easily understandable manner. This requires eloquence – the ability to reach out and persuade even difficult individuals. Communication skills also involve correctly interpreting other people's messages. This includes listening keenly, decoding signals such as facial expressions, gestures, and posture, and reacting accordingly. The search for creating mutual benefits

Table 1.1.   Success factors in negotiations.

No.	Key Success Attribute	Description
1.	Focus on objectives and efficiency	Time management
2.	Amicable climate and relationships	Relationship management
3.	Assurance of balance in power	Power management with equality and reciprocity
4.	Creation of mutual understanding	Communication management
5.	Creation of mutual benefits	Fairness and openness
6.	Formulation of realistic objectives	Clarity and transparency
7.	Focus on results and additional benefits	Results management and value enrichment

is imperative. Targets in negotiations must be clearly defined and transparent, with minimum and maximum values set for each category. In practical terms, this means two separate demands must be set in a range, a minimum objective (minmum position) and a maximum objective (maximum position). The A-6 negotiation framework is a procedural and logical negotiation approach. It focuses on value creation and results orientation through tried and tested negotiation techniques, innovative tools, and modern concepts.

1.4 Agile and Situational Negotiation

Agile companies can adapt their organisation and business model to new market requirements in a short period of time (Kleemann, 2020). In addition, agile negotiation teams and concepts are proactive in seizing opportunities as they arise. This applies to all areas of the company and its various functions. Agility within the company is the right mix of "doing agile" (methods) and "being agile" (mindset). In addition to adapting the negotiation process, agility includes choosing agile and different negotiation media such as offline and online communication through telephone, email, etc. (Nowotny, 2017). Agile and situational negotiations are scenarios in which the negotiator adapts their negotiation style and activities to align with the specific situation and climate they face. This is the most flexible and efficient way to conduct a negotiation. In situational negotiations, the negotiator analyses and interprets the characteristics and goals of the other parties and then chooses the negotiation type that offers the greatest benefit. This is a flexible and dynamic negotiation style because it can be modified according to the circumstances that arise. The negotiator must know the characteristics of the negotiation very well before taking a position. In this sense, a large flow of information between the parties is necessary so that the objectives of each party and their respective points of resistance (defined in distributive negotiations) can be identified. Among the primary characteristics of this negotiation style, we can highlight the following:

- It is necessary to be aware of the strengths and weaknesses of the other party in order to adapt the negotiation style.
- In order to make a decision, the personal relationship with the other party must be evaluated.

- The solutions to one or more problems can be negotiated.
- It is a negotiation in which characteristics can dynamically change over time and throughout the process.
- The situation of both parties is known.
- The negotiator must be trained to adapt to every negotiation style.

1.5 Tips and Tricks for Successful Negotiations

1.5.1 *Professionalism and skills*

Effective negotiation management requires that negotiation be understood as a joint problem-solving and decision-making process rather than a purely adversarial battle for distribution or argumentation. In addition, solutions must be sought to optimally expand the solution space. It is therefore necessary for negotiators to act professionally and possess specific negotiation skills. People exhibit different cognitive characteristics when certain influences (e.g., relationship, trust, and sympathy) are present. In addition, they may prefer different styles of engagement (competitive, collaborative, compromising, evasive, accommodative, etc.). However, through targeted training, other conflict styles can also be learned (Abdel-Latif, 2015). Numerous studies show that training in rational negotiation leads to substantial improvements in negotiation performance. This competence cannot be achieved through classic forms of learning alone. The combination of a structural framework and reflection on one's own experiences based on this framework is also necessary. Negotiation simulations also play an important role in developing negotiation skills (Weh, 2017). Without such a framework, even decades of negotiation experience may lead to suboptimal results.

1.5.2 *Avoid loss of face and open arguments*

Choosing an appropriate negotiation strategy requires clarity in knowing one's own objectives (stating goals and priorities) and the goals of those on the other side (assessing the other side). The basic principle of every strategy should be the principle of avoiding any loss of face. Open arguments should be avoided at all costs. In situations such as outbursts of anger or loss of face, negotiations should be temporarily interrupted to calm the waters.

> **Practical tip:** Take worthwhile breaks when emotions become too strong or one negotiating side is in danger of losing face. Try to calm down emotional negotiators.

1.5.3 *Allocation of negotiation roles*

Negotiations between companies often take place in teams from different functional areas or departments. Basically, all team-based negotiations resemble strategic games to some extent. Every negotiating team needs to clearly allocate roles (Fetsch, 2006). To ensure that all departments and functions are properly considered. A valuable tool is the so-called "negotiation rehearsal", in which negotiation teams practise an upcoming negotiation using all available materials and resources. However, you must also consider what kind of negotiation is being conducted and what role each participant plays. According to the negotiation framework, the following roles exist in negotiations:

- main negotiator (decision-maker),
- specialists and experts (supporters),
- observers (minute takers),
- moderators (facilitators),
- mediators (icebreakers or connectors),
- listeners (people not involved),
- critics (resisters),
- undercover agents (double agents).

The main negotiator or decision-maker is the individual who, exercising their formal authority, approves or rejects negotiation proposals and options. This individual sets negotiation goals, influences the negotiations, and usually also leads them. In some cases, the main negotiator may also act in the background and appoint a deputy to lead the negotiations. In most cases, budget managers or department managers play this role since their position authorises them to make important decisions.

Specialists are experts who support the main negotiator with their specialised knowledge. Experts can estimate the consequences a proposal will have for the negotiation outcome, drawing from their experience.

Observers, as recorders, are not actively involved in the negotiations but document the negotiations and results.

Moderators (facilitators) ensure informal exchange during negotiations (e.g., invisible diplomacy before negotiations) and the creation of a professional negotiating climate. Facilitators are usually impartial and help with the investigation and analysis of the facts. Moderators often represent third parties (external consultants) and serve as methodological trainers or mediators, who observe and support the negotiations.

Mediators (icebreakers, connectors) participate in negotiations when parties harden their stances. They serve as icebreakers and connectors who smooth the waves. Mediators are usually appointed by the decision-maker due to their skills and relationships, which make them ideal for mediating when positions have become rigid.

Listeners are non-participating parties without a specific role. They are often clerical staff who may only take part in negotiations in order to provide information when necessary.

Critics (resisters) are individuals belonging to their own camp or that of the negotiating opponents who are critical of the issues at hand and express their concerns openly or covertly. They are seen as individuals who express concerns and show open or hidden resistance. Resistance must be broken during negotiations.

Undercover agents (or double agents) are individuals who act on the other side of a negotiation, covertly providing information to their own side. They are trustworthy and can provide valuable information about the mood, climate, or intentions.

Other negotiation models suggest the following additional personality types that can be recognised during negotiations (Hindle, 1998):

- a negotiator who maintains an overview, occasionally engages others, and uses the team members in a targeted manner;
- a so-called "good" negotiator (or "good cop"), who acts as an identification and leading figure;
- a "bad" and emotional negotiator (or "bad cop"), who gives the other side the impression that it is better not to mess with him;
- the so-called hardliner, who is uncompromising on all issues and whose judgement the team members often bow to;
- the icebreaker, who acts as a moderator and problem solver and thus takes up and brings together the different views;
- the observer, who observes and documents the different views but does not intervene in the proceedings.

These roles help to control negotiations and do not necessarily need to be filled by separate participants. It is only important (above all!) to determine the distribution of roles beforehand in order to avoid friction and maintain a clear direction.

1.5.4 *Appearances play a central role*

Above all, negotiation teams must be aware of the fact that first impressions are of central importance for the success of negotiations. Therefore, companies should not underestimate the importance of appearances. Appearances include seating arrangements, attire, body language, and venue. In addition to these, the negotiation environment should also be carefully considered. In certain countries, negotiations are frequently conducted over communal dinners or with family members present.

1.5.5 *Instructions and systematic negotiation preparation*

To avoid contradictions and inconsistencies, all team members must be carefully instructed (Schranner, 2009). For example, if the team leader explains that he is authorised to negotiate prices but the hardliner later says that they need to consult with company management regarding those prices, it seriously undermines the team's credibility.

1.5.6 *Constructive emotionality*

Every strategy requires that you know exactly the strengths and weaknesses of the members of your own team so that you can use them effectively. But that also means that you must know how many participants your negotiation team needs. In addition, you need to clarify whether all participants need to be present during all negotiations.

Practical tip: Use emotions consciously and purposefully in your strategies and tactics.

1.5.7 *Never lose sight of the goal*

Negotiations usually involve more than just one goal. In business transactions between companies, there are usually several (sub-)goals. In addition to price, these may also include delivery times, quality, capacities, and logistics aspects. The basic requirement for a successful negotiation is to have your own goal and sub-goals in mind. It is important to have dynamic goals and objectives. Minimum objectives represent the lower range, maximum the higher outcome in negotiations. Establishing a clear hierarchy will help to make minimum and maximum goals and objectives transparent (Polwin-Plass, 2016).

1.5.8 *Using strategies and tactics correctly*

Successful negotiation also requires the ability to use different negotiation strategies. Negotiation strategies can be integrative or confrontational (Helmold, 2023). However, this does not mean that integrative strategies are not geared towards confrontational elements. Defending against confrontational behaviour is actually an essential part of an integrative strategy. The following strategies can be used during negotiations:

- *Attack strategy*: The attack strategy is a confrontational strategy used in negotiations. Confrontational negotiations are usually conducted from an assumed (supposed) position of strength, which is defined as largely independent of the market or as a dominant position. From this negotiating position, one can achieve quick results that are higher and superior to the usual conditions and demands. The dominant side accepts that this will permanently damage their relationship with the negotiating partner. The attack strategy is harming the relationship as it is grounded on pressure. This strategy should only be pursued, if there are no other alternatives.
- *Offensive strategy*: An offensive strategy attempts to limit the scope of negotiation. The limitation is usually backed up with statements, price constraints, deadlines, or warnings. In some situations, threatening gestures may also be used. This strategy is often used with supposedly weaker negotiating partners. By defining the negotiation position at the outset, the opposing side is forced to make moves within the scope of the negotiation offered. Often, negotiators pursue this offensive strategy for a potential superior position to achieve their goals.
- *Defensive strategy*: This strategy aims to prevent the negotiation opponents from scoring and achieving their negotiation objectives. Traditionally Defence Negotiations are grounded on persuasion, arguments and the separation of facts from perception.

- *Strategy of small steps (salami tactic)*: If a negotiation involves multiple transactions, a recommended strategy is to separate individual outcomes and balance them against each other. This does not assume a "big hit", but rather small gains that are constantly offset. The strategy of small steps is particularly recommended for difficult negotiators or negotiations, especially when the threat of negotiations failing looms large.
- *Consensus strategy*: This strategy focuses on reaching a compromise for all parties, where one works on a partnership-focused solution.
- *Rational problem-solving strategy*: This strategy focuses on reaching a compromise for all parties based on objective facts, data, and solutions. The effects and outcomes of negotiations are quantified in numerical details and figures.

1.5.9 *Using anchoring effects correctly*

In negotiations, initial proposals act as so-called "anchors" when the information contained in the first proposal systematically influences the course of the negotiation and the final result (Northcraft and Neale, 1987). The anchoring effect, which is a concept from cognitive psychology, describes how people are unknowingly influenced by environmental information when making decisions. Environmental information is referred to as the "anchor" that guides the decision and can have an influence even if it is actually irrelevant to the decision. The result is a systematic distortion in the direction of the anchor (Loschilder and Trötschel, 2013). The distorting influence of anchors is not limited to judgements made by uninformed laypersons or naive participants in the laboratory – it is a common, widespread phenomenon (Mussweiler and Strack, 2000). The judgements of experts with many years of professional experience can also be subject to systematic distortions by anchors. For example, both real estate agents with 10 years of professional experience in assessing property values (Northcraft and Neale, 1987) and judges with 10–15 years of professional experience in determining the level of penalty did not adequately adjust their judgements under the influence of an arbitrarily presented number. As a result, high anchors systematically distorted the estimates of real estate agents (and judges), leading to higher price estimates of a property (and higher penalties).

Practical tip: Your *first or second proposal* in a negotiation may serve as an *anchor*. In particular, in negotiations involving only one item, it is advisable to make an *ambitious and, at the same time, precise first proposal*. In order to protect yourself from this robust anchor influence, detailed preparation and research should be carried out before the start of the negotiation, and during the negotiation, the perspective of the other party should be taken into account, with particular attention to their limits.

Practical tips

1. Conduct negotiations professionally in a team. Increase the skills of your employees and negotiators through development and training.

2. Define your strategies and apply them in a targeted manner. Think about the relationship level in each strategy.

3. Rehearse your negotiations as part of negotiation preparation. Good preparation is half the battle.

4. Before every negotiation, build a proper goal hierarchy with a checklist. Articulate and formulate your expectations and goals in the negotiation clearly and transparently. For example, a goal hierarchy could look like this:

   - Maximum goal: price reduction of 8% for the 2024, 2025, and 2026 financial years.
   - Minimum goal: price reduction of 4% for the 2024, 2025, and 2026 financial years.
   - Intermediate goal: price reduction scale of 4–6% for the 2024, 2025, and 2026 financial years, then postpone the negotiation with a further target of 8% depending on the business situation.

Prioritise your goals. Define the minimum and maximum targets in each category.

References

Abdel-Latif, A. (2015). Nicht verblüffen lassen. Schützen Sie sich vor den zehn dreckigsten Verhandlungsfallen. Available at: https://www.focus.de/finanzen/experten/adel_abdel-latif/nicht-bluffen-lassen-schuetzen-sie-sich-vor-den-zehn-dreckigsten-verhandlungsfallen_id_4772172.html [Accessed on 6 July 2022].

Fetsch, F. R. (2006). *Verhandeln in Konflikten: Grundlagen – Theorie – Praxis* (German edition). Wiesbaden: Verlag für Sozialwissenschaften.

Helmold, M. (2022). *Leadership. Agile, virtuelle und globale Führungskonzepte in Zeiten von neuen Megatrends*. Cham: Springer.

Helmold, M. (2023). *Verhandlungen gewinnen. Konzepte, Methoden und. Tools*. Wiesbaden: Springer.

Helmold, M., Tracy, D., and Hummel, F. (2022). *Successful Negotiations: Best-in-Class Recommendations for Breakthrough Negotiations*. Wiesbaden: Springer.

Hindle, T. (1998). *Negotiating Skills (Essential Managers)*. London: Dorling Kindersley.

Kleemann, F. (2020). *Agiler Einkauf: Mit Scrum, Design Thinking & Co. die Beschaffung verändern*. Wiesbaden: Springer.

Kraus, H. J. (2022). *Verhandlungsführung. Schnelleinstieg für Architekten und Bauingenieure*. Wiesbaden: Springer.

Loschilder, D. and Trötschel, R. (2013). Der Verhandlungsbeginn – Wer startet, wann (nicht), und wie in eine Verhandlung? *The Inquisitive Mind*. Available at: https://de.in-mind.org/article/der-verhandlungsbeginn-wer-startet-wann-nicht-und-wie-in-eine-verhandlung?page=2 [February 2013].

Mussweiler, T. and Strack, F. (2000). The use of category and exemplar knowledge in the solution of anchoring tasks. *Journal of Personality and Social Psychology*, 78(6), 1038–1052.

Northcraft, G. B. and Neale, M. A. (1987). Experts, amateurs, and real estate: An anchoring-and-adjustment perspective on property pricing decisions. *Organizational Behavior and Human Decision Processes*, 39(1), 84–97.

Nowotny, V. (2017). *Agil verhandeln mit Telefon, E-Mail, Video, Chat & Co. Die Toolbox mit Strategien, Verhaltenstipps und Erfolgsfaktoren*. Stuttgart: Schäfer-Pöschel.

O'Brien, J. (2016). *Negotiations for Procurement Professionals*, 2nd edn. Croyden: Kogan Page.

Polwin-Plass, L. (2016). Checklisten für den Vertrieb. Verhandlungsstrategie. *Die Vertriebszeitung*. 22 September 2016. Available at: https://vertriebszeitung.de/verhandeln-im-grenzbereich-strategien-und-taktiken-im-vertrieb/ [Accessed on 20 March 2018].

Schranner, M. (2009). *Verhandeln im Grenzbereich. Strategien und Taktiken für schwierige Fälle*, 8. Auflage. München: Econ.

Schranner, M. (2015). 7 Prinzipien für erfolgreiches Verhandeln. BME-Keynote Matthias Schranner gibt sieben Tipps für zielführende Verhandlungen. 15 January 2015 [Accessed on 20 March 2018].

Weh, F. (2017). Tarifverhandlungen Wege zur Konfliktvermeidung. *Institut der deutschen Wirtschaft*. Available at: https://www.iwkoeln.de/studien/hagen-lesch-mehr-professionalitaet-weniger-eskalation.html [Accessed on 6 July 2022].

Weiss, J.N. (2022). *Verhandlungen in der Praxis: Erfolgreiche Strategien aus Wirtschaft, Politik und dem täglichen Leben.* Weinheim: Wiley.

Chapter 2

Negotiate Like Your Life Depends on It

2.1 Moving the Power Balance to Your Own Advantage

The key success factor in negotiations is increasing the power balance between parties. Figure 2.1 shows that alternatives, information, urgency, and importance are important factors for one's value creation and negotiation position (Helmold, 2023). Bargaining power refers to the relative ability of parties in an argumentative situation (such as bargaining, contract writing, or drafting an agreement) to exert influence on one another and secure favourable terms in an agreement.

This power derives from various factors, such as each party's alternatives to the current deal, the value of what is being negotiated, and the

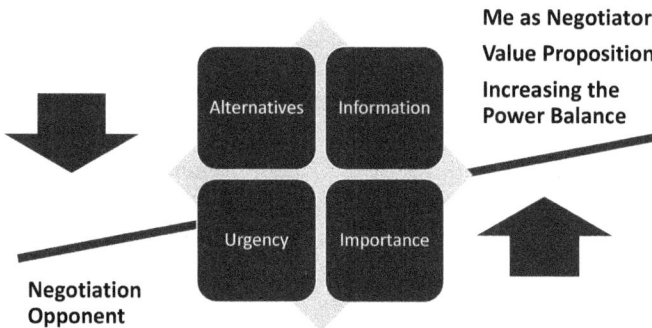

Figure 2.1. Increasing one's power balance.

17

urgency of reaching an agreement (Haberfeld, 2022). A party's bargaining power can significantly shift the outcome of negotiations, leading to more advantageous positions for those who possess greater leverage.

2.2 Mental and Physical Strength

If you want to conduct difficult negotiations successfully, you have to bring in your full potential: be physically healthy, stay calm yet committed, exercise critical judgement, maintain emotional control, and, above all, remain positively motivated. An affirmative, optimistic attitude often conveys self-confidence and sympathy (Schranner, 2020). For your mental attitude, it is important to keep your negotiation goal in mind and concentrate on it. Success in negotiations is also based on a convincing manner of presentation and compelling arguments.

2.3 Cognitive and Affective Empathy

Both cognitive and affective empathy play a central role in negotiations. You must be able to recognise the emotions and stress-related changes in your negotiating partner and actively respond to them. If you, as a negotiator, want your counterpart to change their mind, you need to understand their motives, feelings, and behaviours. Empathy is exactly that: the art of reading between the lines, justifying another person's perspective, and reacting accordingly. Negotiations are not always about rational decisions. Successful negotiators need the ability to use tactical empathy in a targeted manner in order to steer their counterpart's behaviour in the desired direction and ultimately emerge from the negotiation as winners (Hofmann, 2018). In addition to observing and decoding body language and micro expressions, an important aspect is affective empathy. How can you respond to a negotiating partner's emotions and needs? Empathy in negotiations is about both parties. In negotiations, you need a trusting relationship in order to get through to your opponent, gain insights about their arguments, reasons, and motives, recognise your pain threshold during the negotiation, and ultimately be successful in the negotiation. You need a good relationship and empathy for the other person to open up at all. In addition, both types of empathy are critical to success and crucial for successful negotiation.

2.4 Bring about Stressful Situations and Conflicts Depending on the Situation

2.4.1 *Create stressful situations*

Most negotiations in purchasing are characterised by stressful situations. When stress levels increase, structure and overview are often lost, making it difficult to objectively evaluate numbers and offers. Especially when stress occurs, tactics may no longer be adapted to the situation (Abdel-Latif, 2015). During procurement negotiations, the negotiator, who is under stress, often remains too attached to their preferred solution. A differentiated perception of the various options for a result is no longer possible. This results from mental rigidity under stress, limiting flexibility and creative processes.

2.4.2 *Targeted use of conflict situations*

People in negotiations have to process a lot of information simultaneously and make complex decisions within a short span, systematically influencing the further course of the negotiation. Negotiation trainers usually suggest acting rationally and unemotionally in negotiations. While mild eustress (positive stress) ensures that we are more efficient in decision-making situations, we must be wary of distress (negative stress) during negotiations. This is because if the levels of stress hormones – adrenaline, norepinephrine, and cortisol – increase as the psychological pressure increases, their positive effect is diminished. Stuttering, a lack of concentration, and blackouts are the consequences. The more the brain is under stress, the more it encourages irrational behaviour.

However, modern concepts recommend consciously and purposefully triggering stressful situations. To do this, you can consciously trigger conflicts in order to cause stress for the other side. Stress is designed to prepare the mind and body for fight or flight. When experiencing stress symptoms, the negotiating opponents often lose track and reveal their weak points through thoughtless actions or non-verbal signals.

2.4.3 *Trigger time pressure and set deadlines*

Those who have time on their side often also have the advantage in negotiations. Time pressure automatically leads to stress. Stress can be a powerful tool in negotiations, aimed at significantly restricting the nego-tiating partner's rational (logical) thinking. The conclusion is that serious and expensive mistakes are made, and decisive concessions are often made far too early (Brost, 2017). The trick is often used in two ways:

- Negotiations are scheduled at extremely short notice in order to deprive the other side of the opportunity to prepare optimally.
- The duration of negotiations will be greatly shortened. This is intended to prevent the other side from being able to present its position correctly.

2.4.4 *Initiate bad placement*

Poor seating arrangements and placements can also lead to increased stress during negotiations. As the inviting party, you take a seat in front of the window; the opposing party is seated against the wall. Due to the bright light, they become tired more quickly and experience a decrease in concentration. In addition, they will be able to see and read your gestures and facial expressions only to a limited extent. There are also examples of clients often being seated in lower, uncomfortable chairs. This is intended to subconsciously instill a sense of inferiority.

2.4.5 *Good person, bad person*

This is one of the most well-known, yet still very effective, tricks fre-quently used by both large and small companies. One negotiator plays the "good" person or negotiator (the "good guy"), while the other is the "bad" person (the "bad guy"), whose job is to continuously put the other party under pressure with counterarguments and an arrogant demeanour, con-sciously aiming to cause antipathy. The other party, automatically feeling drawn to the good guy, tends to make concessions.

2.5 The Negotiation Script: Logic and Structure (*Roter Faden – Red Thread, Line*)

The negotiation script, or common thread, refers to the recognisability of the central idea and structure in negotiations. In a quick-witted negotiation team, the goal must be clearly defined; each co-negotiator should know exactly who has to do what and when. If you want to maintain the common thread, you must ensure that both the goal and your team are completely under control during negotiations. Negotiation success hinges on clear objectives, a logical structure, the mental attitude, and the cohesion of the entire team. The structured phase model A-6 is particularly useful, as it also takes into account the different orientations of the negotiating partners.

2.6 Conducting Negotiations: Driver's Seat, Personal Empowerment, and Self-Empowerment

Negotiation experts conduct negotiations from the driver's seat. The position from the driver's seat involves actively moderating and systematically leading the negotiations. (Helmold, 2022). Good preparation, self-confidence, persuasiveness, and open communication are elements of good and targeted negotiations (Rock, 2019).

Besides the aforementioned characteristics, personal empowerment and self-empowerment must be integrated into successful negotiations (Jagodzinska, 2020). Personal empowerment is about taking control of your own life and making positive decisions based on what you want. It's closely linked to attributes such as self-esteem and self-confidence; however, true empowerment comes when you convert intention into action.

2.7 Identification of Non-Verbal Signals

If negotiators want to be successful, they need the ability to actively perceive their counterpart, to decipher their counterparts' body language, choice of words, and tone of voice in order to recognise their true motives and needs. And these are often much more important than what is said verbally. You can read about exactly what you need to pay attention to in body language in my book, *Listen With Your Eyes*. An important aspect is the so-called micro expressions because, unlike normal body language, they cannot be consciously controlled. Micro expressions, easily recognisable by the trained eye, are fleeting facial signals visible for a fraction of a second (40–500 ms), and they all have a neurological trigger. We could all read these micro expressions as children, even before we could speak; we felt how our own mothers felt. Therefore, you learn to use your gut feeling and intuition again.

2.8 Use of Emotional Intelligence

The term "emotional intelligence" (EI) in negotiations refers to the ability to understand one's own feelings and those of others to accurately classify these emotions and derive appropriate actions from them. Basically, EI refers to an acumen in regard to feelings. In his bestseller, Daniel Goleman even went so far as to equate it with the intelligence quotient (Hofmann, 2018). It was important for him not only to be intelligent in the classic sense, i.e., to act purposefully and logically, but also to have emotional intelligence, i.e., perceiving your own feelings as well as others' and reacting to them. EI is a combination of five different competencies:

- **Self-awareness:** consciously perceiving your own emotions.
- **Self-regulation:** controlling and directing impulses from your own emotions.
- **Empathy:** perceiving and understanding other people's feelings.
- **Motivation:** willingness to implement necessary actions.
- **Social skills:** seeing yourself as part of a system, thinking in terms of relationships, and behaving considerately.

2.9 Application of Novel Techniques and AI: Neurolinguistic Programming

Neurolinguistic programming (NLP, for short) is a collection of methods and communication techniques intended to influence psychological processes in people. The term itself is intended to express that brain processes ("neuro-") can be changed with the help of language ("linguistic") on the basis of systematic instructions ("programming"). Nowadays, negotiations can also involve the use of AI. Areas of action include preparing for negotiations, conducting negotiations, and drafting contracts. There are already bots that use AI to negotiate with people. However, until a serious paradigm shift takes hold, we will be dealing with mixed forms in the future: automation and AI on the one hand and, to some extent, the human factor on the other. Contract negotiations can be optimised for the negotiation process using AI-based analytics. Contract analysis tools optimise and accelerate negotiations in the following ways:

- Automatically recommend replacement wording for risky terms in your company's pre-approved clause library.
- Automatically extract clauses and conditions from incoming contracts.

- Classify the risk level of extracted terms by applying logic to create detailed scorecards based on your organisation's legal and business guidelines.

> **Practical tip:** Use the trends, techniques, and tips of the negotiation professionals. Negotiate as if your life depends on it. Be prepared; draw your script, and negotiate always from the driver's seat. Train yourself and your employees in negotiations. Apply professional tools and concepts for a successful breakthrough.

References

Abdel-Latif, A. (2015). Nicht verblüffen lassen. Schützen Sie sich vor den zehn dreckigsten Verhandlungsfallen. Available at: https://www.focus.de/finanzen/experten/adel_abdel-latif/nicht-bluffen-lassen-schuetzen-sie-sich-vor-den-zehn-dreckigsten-verhandlungsfallen_id_4772172.html [Abgerufen am 1 April 2018].

Brost, M. (2017). Verhandlungen. Tipps für eine erfolgreiche Verhandlungsstrategie. Mehr fordern, als man will. Available at: https://www.zeit.de/2017/43/verhandlungen-politik-training-matthias-schranner [Abgerufen am 11 July 2018].

Haberfeld, S. J. (2022). *Power Balance. Increasing Leverage in Negotiations with Federal and State Governments – Lessons Learned from the Native American Experience.* Oklohoma: Oklohoma University Press.

Helmold, M. (2022). *Leadership. Agile, virtuelle und globale Führungskonzepte in Zeiten von neuen Megatrends.* Cham: Springer.

Helmold, M. (2023). *Verhandlungen gewinnen. Konzepte, Methoden und Tools.* Cham: Springer.

Hofmann, (2018). *Das FBI-Prinzip: Verhandlungstaktiken für Gewinner.* München: Ariston.

Jagodzinska, K. (2020). *Negotiation Booster: The Ultimate Self-Empowerment Guide to High Impact Negotiations.* New York: Business Expert Press.

Rock, H. (2019). *Erfolgreiche Verhandlungsführung mit dem Driver-Seat-Konzept.* Wiesbaden: Springer.

Schranner, M. (2020). *Das Schranner-Konzept: Die neuen Prinzipien für die Verhandlungen der Zukunft.* Berlin: Ullsteinverlage.

Chapter 3

Six Steps for Negotiation Breakthrough: The A-6 Negotiation Concept

3.1 Successful Negotiations in Six Steps

The ability to negotiate has long been considered both an ability and a talent of specially trained individuals. The A-6 negotiation concept is a holistic, systematically structured concept consisting of six steps, which describes the entire path from negotiation preparation to agreement in the negotiation process. The phase model forms the basis for negotiation management. Methods such as profiling or case analysis, findings from psychology, cognitive research to control the negotiating partners, strategies to influence negotiating power, and specially developed negotiation techniques that serve to achieve a breakthrough in negotiations are used. In addition to its practical relevance, intercultural aspects are also described in the addendum, which are used in international transactions across various countries. Although the model focuses on business negotiations and transactions, other negotiations, e.g., political negotiations, those involving private individuals, or addressing issues like alimony, can also be carried out within the framework of these six steps.

Negotiations start with analysing objectives, participants, and motives. After a detailed analysis, the selection of appropriate strategies and tactics takes place. The basis here is the script or manuscript, detailed later on. Strategies and tactics determine the argumentation and structure of the negotiations. Once these steps are completed, you can start the actual negotiation. This is where the radius of action is determined. Within the strategy and argumentation, potential counterarguments from the side and

Figure 3.1.   Steps in the A-6 negotiation concept.

resistance are identified, along with tactics for successfully overcoming this resistance while ensuring that the negotiating partner does not lose face. As a final step, the design of the negotiation result and compliance with the negotiation are of crucial importance (Helmold, 2022).

Figure 3.1 shows the six steps, from analysis to respecting and adhering to the agreement.

3.2 Logic and Structure of the A-6 Negotiation Concept

The A-6 negotiation concept is designed in six logically structured steps, which can be divided into analysis (preparation), execution, and conclusion, as shown in Figure 3.2. The time and duration of negotiations must be carefully planned, as should the venue, seating arrangement, and participants. Depending on elements such as scope, the number of participants, or intercultural differences, negotiations can be quite time-consuming and resource-intensive. The analysis is the cornerstone for a successful conclusion of negotiations and can often require up to 80% of the time invested. The execution of the negotiations is usually shorter and amounts to less than 15% of the time invested. An important point here is the intercultural aspects, especially whether negotiations in culturally different countries are well planned. The conclusion of the negotiation is usually relatively short compared to the preparation and execution. Negotiation

A-6 Negotiation Concept (Dr. Marc Helmold)

A-1: Analysis of Negotiation Scope and Negotiation Partners

A-2: Alignment of Negotiation Strategies and Tactics

A-3: Aggregation and Affirmation of Arguments

A-4: Accomplishment and Amplification of Negotiations

A-5: Assertation of Resistance and Attacking Counterarguments

A-6: Administration of Contracts and Agreements

Analysis

Execution

Agreement

Figure 3.2. A-6 negotiation concept.

results must always be recorded and should also be jointly celebrated by all negotiating partners (Helmold, 2022).

3.3 Preparation as the Key Success Factor

Preparation for negotiations – encompassing the definition of objectives, analysis of negotiating opponents, and selection of suitable strategies and tactics – is a central point in numerous negotiation concepts (Helmold, 2022, 2023). However, the preparations differ from concept to concept. The majority of negotiation experts use a structured template, which is intended to enable professional negotiations (O'Brien, 2016). Concepts also often represent the boundaries and the framework that should not be exceeded in negotiations (Schranner, 2009). The art of successful negotiations often lies in implementing one's own negotiation goals and wishes as much as possible during discussions with the negotiating opponent using suitable strategies, tactics, and tools (Knapp, 2019). Companies therefore usually look for assertive managers and negotiators. Due to the fact that many negotiation concepts and negotiators are impractical and overly theoretical, the A-6 negotiation manuscript, as shown in Figure 3.3, was developed. Dr. Helmold developed the negotiation manuscript in 2015 due to a lack of practical templates for business negotiations.

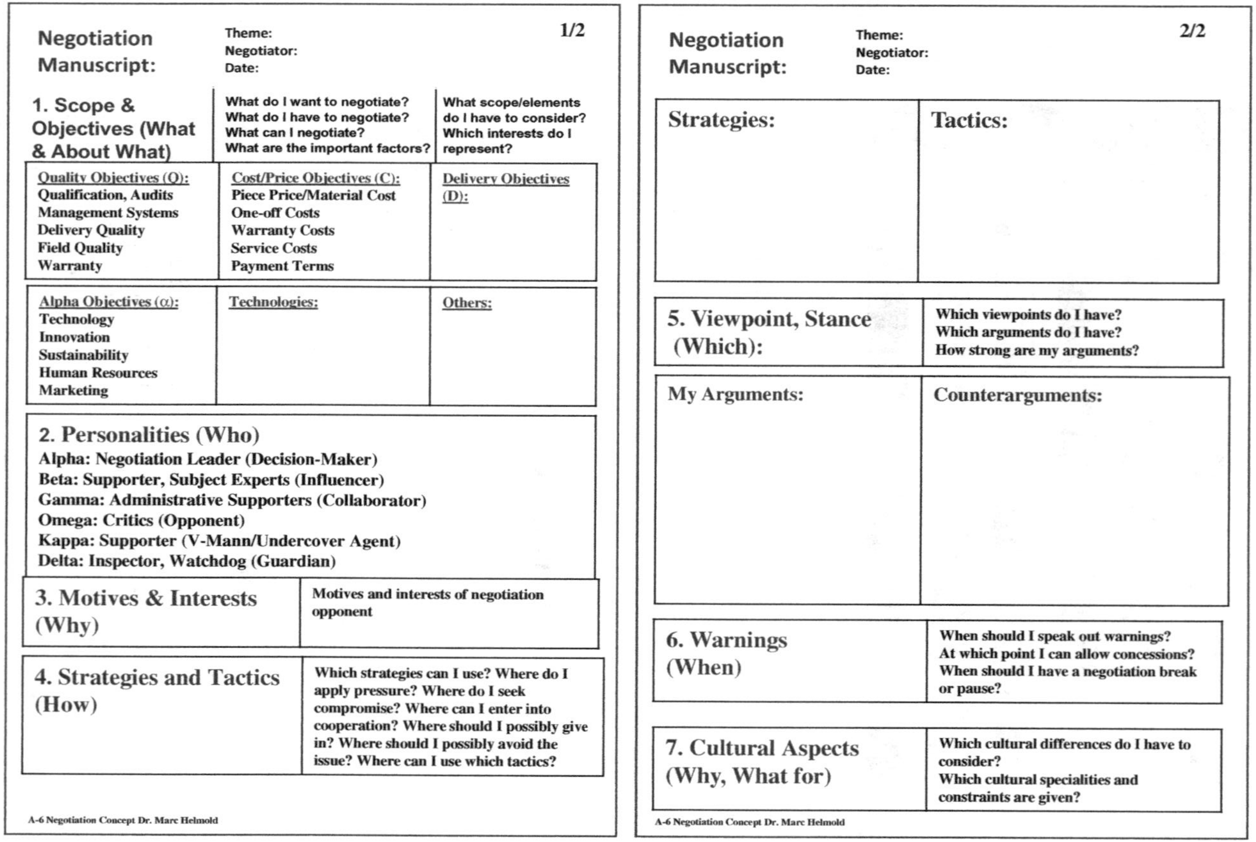

Negotiation Manuscript:
Theme:
Negotiator:
Date:
1/2

1. Scope & Objectives (What & About What)

What do I want to negotiate? What do I have to negotiate? What can I negotiate? What are the important factors? What scope/elements do I have to consider? Which interests do I represent?

Quality Objectives (Q):
Qualification, Audits
Management Systems
Delivery Quality
Field Quality
Warranty

Cost/Price Objectives (C):
Piece Price/Material Cost
One-off Costs
Warranty Costs
Service Costs
Payment Terms

Delivery Objectives (D):

Alpha Objectives (α):
Technology
Innovation
Sustainability
Human Resources
Marketing

Technologies:

Others:

2. Personalities (Who)
Alpha: Negotiation Leader (Decision-Maker)
Beta: Supporter, Subject Experts (Influencer)
Gamma: Administrative Supporters (Collaborator)
Omega: Critics (Opponent)
Kappa: Supporter (Y-Mann/Undercover Agent)
Delta: Inspector, Watchdog (Guardian)

3. Motives & Interests (Why)
Motives and interests of negotiation opponent

4. Strategies and Tactics (How)
Which strategies can I use? Where do I apply pressure? Where do I seek compromise? Where can I enter into cooperation? Where should I possibly give in? Where should I possibly avoid the issue? Where can I use which tactics?

A-6 Negotiation Concept Dr. Marc Helmold

Negotiation Manuscript:
Theme:
Negotiator:
Date:
2/2

Strategies:

Tactics:

5. Viewpoint, Stance (Which):
Which viewpoints do I have?
Which arguments do I have?
How strong are my arguments?

My Arguments:

Counterarguments:

6. Warnings (When)
When should I speak out warnings?
At which point I can allow concessions?
When should I have a negotiation break or pause?

7. Cultural Aspects (Why, What for)
Which cultural differences do I have to consider?
Which cultural specialities and constraints are given?

A-6 Negotiation Concept Dr. Marc Helmold

Figure 3.3. The A-6 negotiation manuscript.

In addition, the A-6 negotiation manuscript has been supplemented with key points on international negotiations, such as cultural peculiarities. As a systematic and logically structured concept, the W-questions (what, why, who, how, etc.) help to ideally structure and implement negotiation processes. The A-6 negotiation manuscript is continually being improved, enabling negotiators to conduct negotiations professionally.

3.4 The Model for Practitioners

Negotiation is a strategic and target-oriented discussion between two parties to resolve an issue that both find acceptable. Negotiations occur between buyers and sellers, employers and prospective employees, or the governments of two or more countries. Successful negotiations typically involve compromises by one or all parties (Helmold, 2023).

The A-6 negotiation concept is the ideal model for practitioners that is easy to learn and implement. This was developed between 2014 and 2016 by Dr. Marc Helmold, who worked as managing director of a market leader in railway and aircraft construction in Asia-Pacific and Europe. This concept has proved itself in numerous international negotiations. The concept shines through its logic and simplicity and is widely applied in practice. The concept for practitioners has been presented to the general public through books, conferences, courses, seminars, and scientific articles. Due to its standardised application, the A-6 negotiation concept has numerous unique selling points (Helmold *et al.*, 2022).

3.5 Effective Tips for Successful Negotiation

In summary, the A-6 negotiation concept represents an ideal framework for international negotiations. The systematic, structured, and transparent approach in six successive steps enables users to conduct negotiations successfully and achieve a negotiation breakthrough. It integrates both intercultural recommendations and practical tips for negotiations and is unique in its form within the field of negotiation models. The valuable recommendations for action link practical and conceptual aspects, specifically in terms of cultural and theoretical components, based on demonstrable negotiation sequences and successfully completed projects. The practical relevance is the focus of the A-6 negotiation concept, with concrete experience enabling a concise and understandable presentation of the content with numerous practical examples. In addition to the practical examples, the framework includes many country-specific recommendations for action, thereby providing the negotiator with numerous unique selling points. Negotiations must be conducted in a structured manner, as suggested by numerous experts and authors. This aspect should be taken into account, particularly in international negotiations, in order to avoid making mistakes in intercultural negotiations. Dr. Marc Helmold's A-6 is a tried-and-tested model that has been used frequently in practice.

Table 3.1 shows a summary of the most important recommendations. The A-6 concept is a sophisticated, systematic negotiation model featuring numerous tried-and-tested and complementary tools requiring holistic application. Training for all employees, both directly and indirectly involved in the negotiations, must be carried out before the negotiations. For employees at the beginning of their careers, it is advisable to have internal negotiation experts on hand to advise them. Detailed negotiation preparation, with analysis of the negotiating scope, determination of responsibilities, and identification of the other side's motives and motivations, is of central importance for achieving a breakthrough in negotiations. When conducting negotiations, motives and not positions should be questioned in order to understand the motives and behaviour of the negotiating opponent and to act accordingly. There are strategies and tactics for conducting negotiations that can be used while taking intercultural

Table 3.1. Six steps for negotiation breakthrough and success.

Phase and Duration	Step	Description
Analyse (Up to 80% of the time)	A-1	Analysis of the negotiating partners and determination of the starting position
	A-2	Selection of suitable strategies and tactics
	A-3	Structure and argumentation of the negotiations
Execution (Up to 15%)	A-4	Execution of the negotiations (negotiation management)
	A-5	Defence against counterarguments and combating resistance
Finalisation & Closing (Up to 5%)	A-6	Design of the negotiation results and contracts

peculiarities into account. It is crucial to focus your argument on the decision-makers and influencers using professional questioning techniques and concise formulations. Non-verbal signals and their patterns indicate whether negotiations are successful or not. At the end of a negotiation, the contract and agreements should be ceremoniously adopted in accordance with the minutes.

References

Helmold, M. (2022). *Leadership. Agile, virtuelle und globale Führungskonzepte in Zeiten von neuen Megatrends.* Cham: Springer.

Helmold, M. (2023). *Verhandlungen gewinnen. Konzepte, Methoden und Tools.* Wiesbaden: Springer.

Helmold, M., Tracy, D., and Hummel, F. (2019). *Erfolgreiche Verhandlungen. Best-in-Class Empfehlungen für den Verhandlungsdurchbruch.* Cham: Springer.

Helmold, M., Tracy, D., and Hummel, F. (2022). *Successful Negotiations: Best-in-Class Recommendations for Breakthrough Negotiations.* Wiesbaden: Springer.

Knapp, P. (2019). *Verhandlungs-Tools: Effiziente Verhandlungstechniken im Business-Alltag.* Bonn: ManagerSeminare Verlags GmbH.

O'Brien, J. (2016). *Negotiations for Procurement Professionals*, 2nd edn. Croyden: Kogan Page.

Schranner, M. (2009). *Verhandeln im Grenzbereich. Strategien und Taktiken für schwierige Fälle*, 8. Auflage. München: Econ.

Chapter 4

Negotiation Preparation and Situation Analysis as the Key to Success (A-1)

4.1 Situation Analysis as the Key Success Factor in Deals and Negotiations

Negotiations are forms of communication between two or more parties about a controversial issue. Negotiations are also characterised by opposing goals, interests, and motives that the parties involved wish to assert for

Figure 4.1. A-6 Negotiation preparation and situation analysis.

themselves. A central point, in this sense, is the situation analysis, with the first three phases as shown in Figure 4.1. Situation analysis includes the analysis of the negotiating partners and determination of the starting position (phase A-1), the selection of suitable strategies (phase A-2), and the development of a logical and structured basis for argumentation (phase A-3) (Helmold, 2023). Important questions within the situation analysis are as follows:

- What scope am I negotiating? How important are the different scopes?
- What are my minimum and maximum goals in each category?
- Who am I negotiating with? Who is the decision-maker? Who are the influencers?
- Who can help me on the other side?
- What target corridors (MaxPo – Maximum Position, MinP – Minimum Position) do I have?
- What goals does my negotiating partner have?
- What motives do my negotiation partners have?
- What interests are there in the respective functions?
- What strategies and tactics will help me succeed in the negotiation?
- What strategies does my negotiation partner use?
- When must there be either a negotiation result or, at least, a partial result?
- Where do I negotiate? Where does my negotiation partner want to conduct the negotiation?
- When should I warn my negotiating opponent?
- What intercultural pitfalls or peculiarities are there?

4.2 Commercial Business Negotiations: B2B, B2C, and B2A

As part of the situation analysis in commercial business negotiations, it is imperative to understand who you are negotiating with. Negotiation opportunities arise in the context of a business relationship between companies in business-to-business (B2B, company–company), business-to-customer (B2C, company–consumer), and business-to-administration (B2A, company–public administration), and vice versa. In B2B transactions, negotiations take place between two or more companies in a national or international context, for example, between a manufacturer and a customer who further processes the purchased materials. In B2C transactions, a company sells its products and services directly to the (end) customer. Negotiations also take place here. In business-to-administration, there are negotiations in public tenders, e.g., the construction of a school.

4.3 Scope of Negotiations (QKL Plus Alpha Method)

Negotiations in business transactions can usually be divided into commercial and technical aspects (Helmold *et al.*, 2022). The scope of negotiations can be complex and diverse; therefore, it must be precisely identified and specified. Technical aspects include, for example, mechanical values, gap dimensions, or other qualitative performance characteristics. Commercial aspects, therefore, relate to topics such as price, delivery date, or insurance of goods in international transactions. In business negotiations, the scope of negotiations can be well integrated into the QKL Plus Alpha concept (Figure 4.2). Q stands for quality, K stands for cost and price, L stands for deliveries, and Alpha includes all other aspects, as follows:

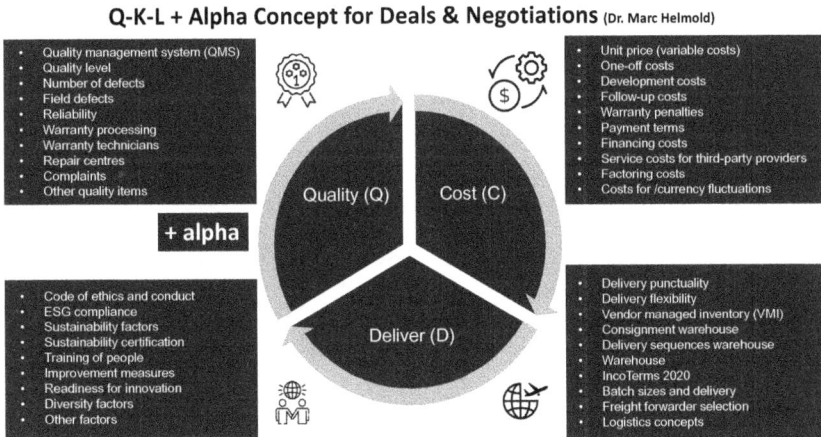

Q-K-L + Alpha Concept for Deals & Negotiations (Dr. Marc Helmold)

Quality (Q)
- Quality management system (QMS)
- Quality level
- Number of defects
- Field defects
- Reliability
- Warranty processing
- Warranty technicians
- Repair centres
- Complaints
- Other quality items

Cost (C)
- Unit price (variable costs)
- One-off costs
- Development costs
- Follow-up costs
- Warranty penalties
- Payment terms
- Financing costs
- Service costs for third-party providers
- Factoring costs
- Costs for /currency fluctuations

+ alpha
- Code of ethics and conduct
- ESG compliance
- Sustainability factors
- Sustainability certification
- Training of people
- Improvement measures
- Readiness for innovation
- Diversity factors
- Other factors

Deliver (D)
- Delivery punctuality
- Delivery flexibility
- Vendor managed inventory (VMI)
- Consignment warehouse
- Delivery sequences warehouse
- Warehouse
- IncoTerms 2020
- Batch sizes and delivery
- Freight forwarder selection
- Logistics concepts

Figure 4.2.   QKL + Alpha concept.

Quality aspects:

- Quality management system (QMS)
- Quality level
- Number of defects
- Field defects
- Reliability
- Warranty processing
- Warranty technicians
- Repair centres
- Complaints

Costs and price aspects:

- Unit price (variable costs)
- One-off costs
- Development costs
- Follow-up costs, warranty penalties
- Payment terms
- Financing costs
- Service costs for third-party providers
- Factoring costs
- Costs for currency fluctuations

Delivery aspects:

- Delivery punctuality
- Vendor managed inventory (VMI)
- Consignment warehouse
- Delivery sequences warehouse and warehouse
- Incoterms 2020
- Lot sizes and delivery
- Carrier selection
- Logistics concepts

Alpha aspects:

- Code of ethics and conduct
- Sustainability factors
- Sustainability certification

- Training of people
- Improvement measures
- Willingness to innovate
- Diversity factors
- Other factors

4.4 Maximum and Minimum Goals

Negotiations should always have a target corridor with both maximum and minimum results (maximum and minimum goals) in every category to be negotiated. The maximum goal is the desire with the best possible outcome. However, maximum goals cannot be achieved in every category. The minimum goal, or minimum requirement, on the other hand, is the red line. At least, this requirement must be implemented in the relevant category to ensure the negotiation result is still acceptable.

Practical tip: Set your target corridors (min., max.) before negotiations:

- Write down all your goals (price, costs, quality, delivery time, etc.).
- Summarise each goal in one sentence and quantify it.
- Prioritise your goals according to importance (priority matrix).
- Determine those goals for which a compromise is possible.
- Determine those goals for which no compromise is possible.
- Determine those goals that you can do without if necessary.
- If possible, give up all unrealistic goals before the negotiation.

4.5 Motivation, Motives and Interests as a Basis for Conflict Resolution and the Conclusion of Negotiations

A negotiation is a controversial form of discussion in which two or more parties try to find a mutual agreement on the terms or price for a transaction by motivating themselves to achieve their goals (Fetsch, 2006). Motivation involves considering what could lead the negotiating partner to reach an agreement. Various aspects are particularly important in this context. During negotiations, opposing interests and motives initially come together, which are identified as part of the situation analysis and (should be) balanced out during the course of the negotiations. The aim is to conclude the negotiations on terms that both parties agree upon by its end. If this is not possible, the negotiations will either be terminated or deemed to have failed. As a general rule, it is important to conduct and lead negotiations from the driver's seat perspective (Rock, 2023). In theory, two phases of negotiation are usually distinguished:

• conflict management and actual negotiations (conflict resolution);
• negotiation conclusion with the formal conclusion of the contract (deal making).

4.6   Cultural Peculiarities

Negotiations play an important role in business transactions at the international level, and they rarely proceed in a uniform manner. Internationally, complex and special situations often arise, for example, due to different language levels among negotiating parties, intercultural differences, or differing values. Conversations usually take place in English or a third language, often with the help of interpreters. In addition, there are different priorities and time expectations. These aspects are complex and involve significant risks that can result in misunderstandings, loss of time, and frustration. In order to prevent this while simultaneously improving communication and understanding between the negotiating partners, certain rules must be observed. Negotiations can drag on for a long time, particularly in people-oriented cultures such as the Middle East, Asia, or Russia. (Lanz, 2018). Negotiators must also deal with the country itself, as well as its customs and cultural conditions, in order to be successful. Central elements in intercultural business negotiations are as follows:

• Language
• Values
• Norms
• Understanding of equality and diversity
• Religion
• Customs
• Laws
• Understanding of time
• Emotionality and rationality
• Group understanding

4.7 Hidden Costs (Total Cost of Ownership)

The total cost of ownership (TCO, for short) is a methodology suitable for situation analysis during negotiations in order to identify all costs incurred in business transactions in advance and to take a special look at the value of the cost drivers and hidden costs. The aim of the TCO is to identify all costs associated with an investment, from initial setup to disposal, so to speak. The most important basis for further understanding of the TCO calculation is the distinction between two types of costs: direct and indirect costs. Direct costs can be budgeted in a business sense and therefore have a demonstrable effect on the success of the company. In addition to acquisition costs and regular material costs, they include, for example, expenses for contractually agreed maintenance work, work performed by administrators, and training programmes. Indirect costs, on the other hand, do not directly impact a company's success and usually arise from non-productive uses. They, therefore, are difficult to quantify. The reliability of manufacturers and third parties, individual learning times to best use the functions of a new printer, the associated assistance from other employees to inexperienced employees, and downtime of new systems are examples of indirect and hidden costs.

4.8 Personality Types and Rank Dynamics in Negotiations

Company negotiations usually take place with the involvement of different departments and functionaries. Rank dynamics, role distribution, and responsibilities are therefore elementary aspects in negotiations and require a transparent assessment as part of the situation analysis. Central questions in psychology are as follows:

- Who is the leader in negotiations? Who is the budget holder?
- Why does one person take the lead in every group?
- Which formal or informal elements make the leader the leader?
- Who supports the decision-maker and leader?
- Why are there almost always critics or naysayers in groups?
- Why do the masses like to agree with an opinion?

According to the A-6 negotiation concept, there are a total of six personality types in negotiations (Table 4.1).

Table 4.1. Personalities in negotiations.

Type	Greek	Description	Recommendation
Alpha	ἄλφα, Α, α	Decider Decision-Maker	Leader, decision-maker, owner, authorised officer or budget officer. Focus the discussion on the decision-maker, identify his motives and interests.
Beta	βῆτα, Β, β	Influencers Allies Confidants	Subject matter experts, allies, confidants, trustees, or representatives of the decision-maker. Focus the discussion on the decision-maker, his supporters, and influencers.
Gamma	Γάμμα, Γ, γ	Supporters	Minutes takers, secretaries, clerks, followers. Watch the gammas because they could also be/become influencers.
Omega	ὦ μέγα, Ω, ω	Critics Concerned parties	Critics, complainers. Don't focus specifically on omega, but be polite and respectful. Watch the omega when it can be useful.
Delta	Δέλτα, Δ, δ	Guardians Watchdogs Inspectors	Guardians, protectors (finance, controlling, accounting, compliance, HR). Find out who the watchdog is. Convince them with mutual benefits and advantages of deals and transactions.
Kappa	Κάππα, Κ, κ	Undercover agents Spies Informants	Spies, undercover agents, liaison. The undercover agent can help you convince the other side. Must be the winner.

4.8.1 *The decision-maker: Alpha type*

The alpha is the leader in negotiations and thus the formal decision-maker. He has budgetary power and also holds the authority to make and ratify agreements. Alphas must reveal their dominance and authority (Hofert, 2015). Alphas are often easy to recognise by their behaviour, seating order, recognition in the group, or status symbol (Helmold *et al.*, 2019). The alpha needs the beta as a supporter; therefore, the alpha, as a decision-maker, usually regards the beta as an ally in a predominantly positive manner (Helmold *et al.*, 2019). Functionally, the alpha is usually the manager or department head. Negotiations must focus on the alpha.

4.8.2 *The influencer: Beta type*

The beta is an expert or subject matter expert and influences the decision-maker through their know-how and expertise. Betas usually have more detailed knowledge. The leader also places trust in them. Betas are usually allies and influencers of the leader. The focus should be on the decision-maker (alpha) and his or her influencers (betas).

4.8.3 *The follower: Gamma type*

Gammas are usually simple clerks or secretaries who do not have a specific role. It is often difficult to distinguish between gammas and betas or to understand their value, so they should be treated appropriately.

4.8.4 *The critic: Omega type*

In every negotiation, there are sceptics and critics (omegas) on your own side or the other side. Omegas must, therefore, be identified and weeded out from your own side before actual negotiations commence to avoid worsening the negotiation result. Criticism can be expressed internally, but it has no role in negotiations and is counterproductive. Conversely, critics on the other side should be observed closely and treated respectfully but not specially.

4.8.5 *The guardian: Delta type*

Guardians (Delta) are considered watchdogs due to their functional roles (e.g., finance, controlling, ethics, or human resources) and ensure that negotiation results are achieved within the framework of company standards and guidelines. Deltas usually possess very detailed specialist knowledge and must be convinced using data, facts, and detailed explanations.

4.8.6 *The undercover agent: Kappa type*

The Kappa serves as the liaison on the other side and can assist in providing useful information. Liaisons on the other side must be built up through good relationship management so that they are well disposed towards us. Kappas can be praised as competent and experienced in negotiations;

however, they should also be treated with the necessary distance and professionalism. The Kappa must always emerge from negotiations as a "winner" in order to be able to use them further.

> **Practical tip:** Focus your negotiations on the Alpha and his or her influencers. Find out what weaknesses the Alpha has in his or her argumentation.

4.9 Getting to the Zone of Mutual Agreement (ZomA)

A central element in negotiations is the question of whether all negotiating parties are in a zone of mutual agreement (ZomA) on contentious issues. The ZomA is the intellectual area in a negotiation wherein two or more parties may find common ground. Here, the negotiating parties can work towards a common goal and reach a potential agreement that includes at least some of the other parties' ideas.

For example, Figures 4.3 and 4.4 show a positive and negative ZomA. In Figure 4.3, you can see that either the buyer or customer has a maximum position (CMaxPo) of 80,000 euros and a minimum position (CMinPO) of 100,000 euros for the investment in a machine and its purchase. Buyers typically aim for low investment costs, which often result from budget specifications or benchmarks. Therefore, the maximum goal

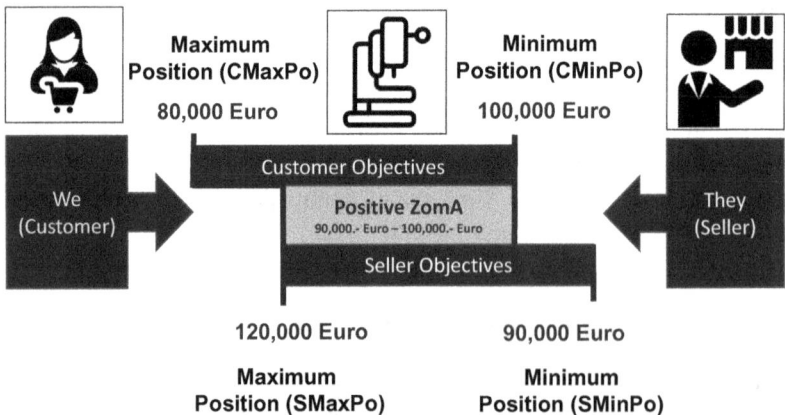

Figure 4.3.   Positive ZomA.

or position is to secure the best purchase price while staying within budget or targets. Often, budget undershoots represent either savings or cost savings for companies. The seller naturally aims for a very high sales price (SMaxPo), with a sales value of 120,000 euros. However, due to the competitive situation, the seller is willing to lower the price and offer discounts. His price limit is 90,000 euros for the machine (SMinPo). If you now compare the two areas, you can see that there is a possible zone of agreement between 90,000 and 100,000 euros. In Figure 4.4, however, you can see that the positions (CMinPo and VMinPo) at 100,000 and 120,000 euros are too far apart, so that no agreement can be reached without some rapprochement.

The scope for negotiation in each category ranges from the minimum to the maximum goal, whereby no element in negotiations should remain completely static. The identification of the scope for negotiation should take place before actual negotiations, as part of optimal preparation (Schmitz *et al.*, 2006). If you have employees and colleagues, they can gauge the other side's reaction to certain negotiation points in advance (Helmold & Terry, 2017). In addition to the maximum and minimum

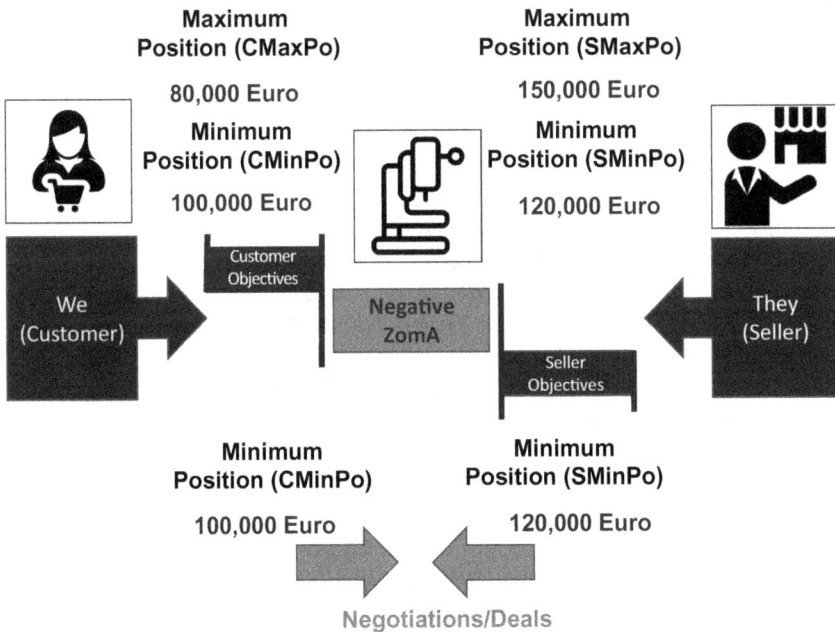

Maximum Position (CMaxPo)
80,000 Euro

Minimum Position (CMinPo)
100,000 Euro

Maximum Position (SMaxPo)
150,000 Euro

Minimum Position (SMinPo)
120,000 Euro

Customer Objectives

We (Customer)

Negative ZomA

They (Seller)

Seller Objectives

Minimum Position (CMinPo)
100,000 Euro

Minimum Position (SMinPo)
120,000 Euro

Negotiations/Deals

Figure 4.4. Negative ZomA.

demands, the point of termination should also be identified in order to show the negotiating parties that the scope for negotiation has been exhausted. Potential added value is also part of sounding out the scope for negotiation. In international negotiations, for example, the price of a supplier may be of secondary importance because they intend to enter the German market with the order or perhaps want to show from a marketing perspective that they have a renowned German customer (Helmold, 2023). Another motive may be to build up a functional logistics network in Europe or Germany, aiming to penetrate the market there. The following aspects are of central importance for identifying the scope:

- Identification of the potential maximum and minimum goals of the negotiating opponent. (What does the other side intend?)
- Are there added values that are attractive to the other side?
- Analysis of possible motives of the other side's participants. (Different departments often have different goals.)
- Who could be used as an influencer? (Are there possible influencers?)
- Identification of possible incentives for the other side. (Which offers are attractive to the other side?)
- What opportunities do I have in each category to be negotiated? (Interests of the other side.)
- Are there constraints on the other side?

References

Fetsch, F. R. (2006). *Verhandeln in Konflikten: Grundlagen – Theorie – Praxis* (German edition). Wiesbaden: Verlag für Sozialwissenschaften.

Fisher, R. and Ury, W. (1981). *Getting to Yes*. London: Penguin Group.

Helmold, M. (2019). *Erfolgreiche Verhandlungen Best-in-Class Empfehlungen für den Verhandlungsdurchbruch*. Wiesbaden: Springer.

Helmold, M. (2023). *Verhandlungen gewinnen. Konzepte, Methoden und Tools*. Wiesbaden: Springer.

Helmold, M. and Terry, B. (2017). *Global Sourcing und Lieferantenmanagement in China*. Berlin: DeGruyter.

Helmold, M., Dathe, T., and Hummel, F. (2022). *Successful Negotiations. Strategies and Tools for the Negotiation Breakthrough*. Cham: Springer.

Hofert, S. (2015). Rangdynamik. Warum Alphas Betas brauchen und Omegas eigentlich nützlich sind. Available at: https://teamworks-gmbh.de/rang dynamik-warum-alphas-betas-brauchen-und-omegas-eigentlich-nuetzlich-sind/ [Abgerufen am 6 June 2022].

Lanz, H. P. (2018). Der Kuchen ist größer als du denkst. *Wirtschaftsmediation* (Frankfurt). Available at: https://www.wirtschaftsmediatoren-ihk.de/f%C3% BCr-hilfesuchende/beitr%C3%A4ge-zum-konfliktmanagement/teil-3-der-kuchen-ist-gr%C3%B6%C3%9Fer-als-du-denkst/ [Abgerufen am 25 March 2018].

Rock, H. (2023). *Successful Negotiation with the Driver-Seat Concept.* Wiesbaden: Springer.

Schmitz, R., Spilker, U., and Schmelzer, J. A. (2006). *Strategische Verhandlungsvorbereitung: Ein Leitfaden mit Arbeitshilfen Wie Sie Ihre Ziele in 5 Schritten sicher erreichen.* Wiesbaden: Springer.

Chapter 5

Negotiation Strategies and Tactics (A-2)

5.1 Strategies and Successful Tactics in the A-6 Negotiation Concept

Negotiation strategies are key to success and ensure a breakthrough in negotiations. Strategic behaviour means concentrating your own potential in such a way that you are superior to your opponent in certain areas that are particularly important for achieving your own goals. That is why the negotiation strategy is always determined in advance of the negotiation based on an analysis of the other side and an assessment of your own negotiation goals. Learning to negotiate correctly also means being able to use different negotiation strategies. The negotiation strategies can be divided into integrative and confrontational strategies. However, that does not mean that integrative strategies are not geared towards confrontational elements. Defending against confrontational behaviour is, in fact, an essential part of an integrative strategy. Professional negotiation distinguishes among five different negotiation strategies (Fig. 5.1):

- Rely on collaboration and partnership.
- Avoid and play for time.
- Make compromises.
- Apply pressure and threats.
- Give in and make concessions.

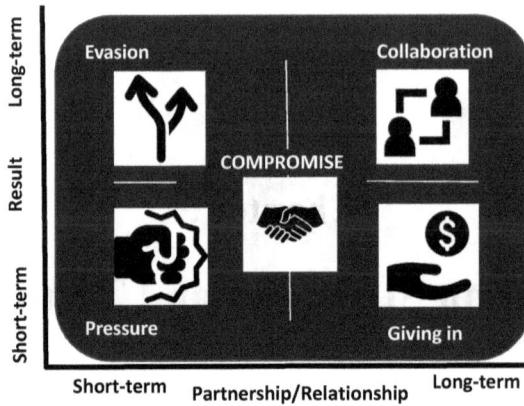

Figure 5.1.   Negotiation strategies.

These strategies set the direction for the approach in a negotiation. They are then implemented using individual tactics.

5.2 Negotiation Strategies

5.2.1 *Applying pressure and threatening*

Applying pressure is often a strategy that is used from a supposed position of strength (Helmold *et al.*, 2022). This negotiation strategy is usually used in situations where the relationship is not so important. Applying pressure can also be used in situations where time is short and a successful negotiation must be achieved (Fetsch, 2006). Anyone using this strategy wants to emerge as the sole "winner" from the negotiation without compromise and is focused on a quick deal. If both negotiating partners choose this type of strategy, a real test of strength and fight quickly ensues. The negotiations then usually fail.

Practical tip: If your negotiation partner uses this strategy, you should ask yourself why they think they can negotiate with you in this way: What possible signal might you have sent to the negotiating partner through your behaviour in advance that they are now building up this enormous pressure in the negotiation and apparently want to win unilaterally?

5.2.2 *Evasion and playing for time*

The evasion strategy involves avoiding confrontation for the time being. Evasion can be useful when you don't have all the information or alternatives to play for time (Helmold, 2023). Consciously avoiding the issue postpones the conflict and can serve as a means of getting into a much better negotiating position at a later point by using the intervening time for the following:

- negotiate with alternatives;
- gain additional time;
- gather information;
- prepare better for the negotiations;
- develop options for action;
- gain information about the negotiating partner's real demands, interests, and motives.

The statements used can be of the following kinds:

- "Do you want to discuss the issue at the next negotiation?"
- "Why don't we discuss it next time?"
- "I have other important appointments."
- "We can't discuss the issue because I'm under time pressure."
- "I would like to negotiate this at another time because I don't want to miss my plane/train."

Practical tip: Don't miss the right time to switch your negotiating strategy! If you stay in avoidance mode for too long, you may end up appearing powerless and weak.

5.2.3 *Make a compromise*

This negotiation strategy is a weakened form of the Harvard, or win-win, concept. Both parties assert some of their interests but give up others. The aim is to resolve conflicts or prevent them from arising in the first place (Fisher and Ury, 1981). Both negotiating partners do not remain in their extreme positions during the negotiation, but they meet more or less in the middle. A compromise can be a possible solution during negotiations if no agreement is reached at all.

The related statements can be of the following forms:

"For further cooperation, I propose the following compromise!"
"This negotiation result has the following mutual advantages for us!"
"To further strengthen our relationship, I make the following suggestion: XXX."

Practical tip: When choosing this basic strategic approach, always be aware that a certain amount of frustration may be triggered on both sides afterwards. Because even though an agreement has been reached, the compromise often leaves a bad aftertaste: It can lead to at least one of the parties fearing that they have carelessly given something away, and the feeling of success might be missing despite the agreement being reached. In the end, neither party may be really satisfied, which does not necessarily make future collaboration easier or more productive.

5.2.4 *Collaboration and partnership*

Collaboration means cooperation and working together based on trust. The basis of the collaboration and partnership strategy is not to act stubbornly, but rather to take the negotiating partner along with you. In order to achieve this and, therefore, establish a long-term successful collaboration, understanding the negotiating partner's point of view precisely is essential. Where do they stand, and what are their needs and wishes? Ask questions, and listen extremely carefully and empathetically without judging or condemning. Find the common ground, and identify the shared history that you already have.

Examples of statements for collaborative strategies are as follows:

- "To further strengthen our relationship, I make the following suggestion XXX."
- "Why don't we cooperate as follows?"
- "In the long term, both partners benefit if we cooperate on this aspect."
- "Cooperation has the following advantages for both parties."

Practical tip: A long-term orientation requires trust. If the necessary basic trust in the negotiating partner is not present, this strategic orientation is extremely dangerous. If the negotiating partner is only interested in quick results and a short-term orientation in their favour, you should refrain from this strategy.

5.2.5 Giving in and making concessions

Giving in is about strategically avoiding conflict and possible damage to the relationship, so that you make concessions and show goodwill. If you plan to give in in advance, you don't need to resort to this strategy as an emergency solution. You are then prepared to accept certain demands or conditions and use these as an opportunity, for example, to get the other party to give in too. A key strategy for success, particularly in international negotiations, is to make concessions where the other party's greatest interests lie. Giving in should include something in return.

Examples of statements for collaborative strategies are as follows:

- "I understand your argument and agree with you."
- "I am happy to agree to your demand, but would expect XXX in return."
- "Your suggestion sounds good, but I would like to make the following suggestion in return."
- "I am very happy to accommodate you, but I also expect concessions from XXX."

Practical tip: Concessions signal a willingness to cooperate. This gives you the opportunity to forgo relatively unimportant demands of your own, allowing you to receive demands from your negotiating partner that are important to you (reciprocity principle).

5.3 Situational Alternative Strategies

5.3.1 Offensive strategy

The offensive strategy (Figure 5.2) is often used with supposedly weaker negotiating partners and bears resemblance to the strategy of exerting pressure. By defining your position at the beginning of the negotiation, the

Figure 5.2.   Situational negotiation strategies.

other side is required to operate solely within the negotiating scope offered. This is achieved throgh direct and short statements. Offensive negotiations strategies mean that you take the initiative and lead the discussion from the driver seat. Offensive negotiations can also include aggresive demands and high-pressure deadlines. Offensive must be balanced and involve concessions, as offensive strategies bear the danger, that the negotiation opponent is withdrawing from the negotiation.

5.3.2 *Defensive strategy*

The defensive strategy is primarily about damage limitation and limiting losses. If the negotiating power of the other side is so great that one can assume certain demands without which no negotiation success can be achieved, then the only option is to look for ways of compensation. Anyone who uses such a strategy merely to remain in a relationship with a larger partner will subsequently be judged in the future based on the concessions they make.

5.3.3 *Strategy of small steps*

If extensive packages are being negotiated, a strategy is recommended in which the volumes are divided up and the partial results achieved are then recorded and weighed against one another before offsetting. This does not assume a major breakthrough but rather small partial successes that are constantly offset against each other. The strategy of small steps is recommended for complex projects.

5.3.4 *Problem-solving strategy*

The problem-solving strategy is based on the use of analyses, data, figures, and facts to conclude negotiations. Focusing on rational data, logistical requirements, or technical problems is a strategy that focuses on topics of mutual interest and defines responsibilities and services from this. The advantage is that neither of the negotiating partners needs to specify the effort required for its implementation, thereby creating an internal swing. However, this strategy is only suitable for negotiating partners who have sufficient capacity on their own.

5.4 Dynamic Application of Suitable Strategies

A negotiation is a process in which several parties want to reach an agreement based on their respective interests and positions. Negotiation strategies and tactics are used for this purpose. Negotiation strategies determine the success of the negotiation and must always be used dynamically and situationally in negotiations (Abdel-Latif, 2015). Negotiation strategies and scenarios – when and where each is most suitable – must be considered as part of the situation analysis. The negotiation strategy not only indicates the direction of the conversation but also determines the entire approach within the negotiation situation. The strategy should always be chosen based on whether long-term cooperation is in sight, or whether it is merely a quick conclusion to the negotiations.

5.5 Tactics in Negotiations

5.5.1 *Useful tactics for practice*

If negotiators want to achieve their goals in negotiations, it is advisable not to rely solely on arguments. Often, only the right strategy and appropriate tactics will help negotiators achieve a breakthrough and required outcome in negotiations. The 10 most suitable tactics, from a practical perspective, are shown in Table 5.1. These 10 useful tactics can be used within the A-6 negotiation concept.

Table 5.1. Tactics for negotiations.

No.	Negotiation Tactics	Description
1.	Driver's seat tactics	Leading the negotiation: determine the timing and use small steps as a tactical element
2.	Bad cop, good cop	Different and opposing roles: the good and bad buyer or seller
3.	Time limit and deadline	Setting a short time limit or setting a "deadline": take it or leave it
4.	Mirroring	The negotiating partners showing empathy
5.	Appeal to a higher authority	"My boss says that…"
6.	Asymmetrical seating arrangement	Irritating the other side
7.	Shared visions	Appeal to the established relationship and its long-term nature
8.	Emotional excitement and surprise	Using emotions with a clear purpose
9.	An eye for an eye	Step by step, making small concessions based on small wins
10.	Flattery and sweet talk	Compliments and gifts

5.5.2 *Sit in the driver's seat and determine the timing*

The topic of time is, therefore, an extremely important point in negotiations – one that you cannot allow your negotiation partners to take control of. If you want to ensure good negotiation results, you should always be the manager of time and topics. Time can be used consciously. Playing for time suggests to the negotiating partner that you have alternative courses of action. This is usually how concessions and allowances are made. In addition to your own timeline, setting up a systematic agenda and sending it to the negotiating partner in advance is advisable. This way, you can determine the time, topics, and process, establishing a clear structure, thus gaining two important advantages:

- The negotiating partner cannot put you under time pressure.
- The negotiating partner cannot put you under pressure or steer you.

With the help of this tool, you are always in the driver's seat and can safely guide the negotiating partner through the process. If they digress during the negotiation, refer to the agenda.

5.5.3 *Good cop, bad cop*

"Good cop, bad cop" is a psychological strategy employed by police officers during interrogations when necessary. The technique is known in the USA, and it has entered popular culture in an exaggerated form as a film cliché. In actual interrogations, it is only used subtly, and it is not well known as a formal technique. However, it can also be used in private negotiations. Two police officers take turns questioning a suspect or witness. The general aim is to generate sympathy for the "good cop" so that he may act as a kind of "confessor".

The "bad cop" uses seemingly unjustified but secretly intended personal attacks against the person being interrogated to provoke and, at the same time, intimidate or even threaten him. This is the basis for the appearance of the good cop. He appears understanding, supportive, and cautious towards the person being interrogated. He tries to build a loose, personal bond. In doing so, he makes it seem, to the person being interrogated, that it will be difficult to protect the person from the attacks of the bad cop. By offering him a coffee, a cigarette, or something similar, an attempt can be made to create a positive attitude towards the good cop. He can also try to grant the accused certain privileges or to morally justify possible actions. The good cop often does not appear during the actual interrogation but only afterwards, in the hallway or a separate lounge, during a kind of "informal interrogation". However, statements made there are just as valuable as those obtained during the actual interrogation. The aim of alternating between provocation and empathy is to get the suspect to confess or elicit certain statements. The bad cop puts the suspect in an emotionally agitated state, while the good cop sells the statement as a way out of a threatening situation. This principle can be used effectively in negotiation and sales situations, and it is also employed as a tactic in such situations.

- In the "good cop, bad cop" method, a salesperson presents himself as a "good guy" who makes the buyer an incredibly good offer that he (allegedly) can hardly explain to his boss.
- The "bad cop" can either be present as an imaginary person in the background, who has to be accountable to the "good cop", or be actually present as a second person, arguing against the "unsustainable" offer of his protagonist.

5.5.4 *Deadline: Setting a time limit*

Setting a deadline leads to a yes or no (take it or leave it) situation and is ideally used when there are alternative courses of action. Not every negotiation is subject to a deadline; however, even if it isn't, using one can exert additional pressure. By setting a time limit on an offer or the entire negotiation, you can force the other party to commit. However, this method of applying pressure only works if you are really prepared to break off the negotiations should there be any doubts. Otherwise, the deadline simply fizzles out without any further effect.

5.5.5 *Mirroring the negotiating partner*

Conducting negotiations successfully doesn't merely mean using the appropriate strategy and possessing well-prepared arguments. A large part of the negotiation is determined solely by interpersonal communication. It is, therefore, worth thinking outside the box to understand how our body language affects negotiations. Mirroring is a simple yet effective technique for negotiations and conflicts. In a conversation, you can mirror body language and approach. I follow my conversation partner in terms of content. If I have the feeling that he is comfortable in the conversation, then I change my behaviour. If he follows me now, he feels comfortable, and we are in sync. It is also called the butterfly dance, i.e., "we are on the same wavelength". My counterpart is now open to me. And only now do I begin to convey my approach. We talk about this and that, and if I change my behaviour, my counterpart follows me. He follows me for a while, but then suddenly, he folds his arms. What do I have to do now? Backtrack, go to where I lost him; catch him again, mirror him a bit, and then continue at a slightly slower pace. That is what it means to mirror someone physically. I can also mirror someone through language, through the speed and pitch of their voice, as well as the dialect. You can also mirror someone linguistically by adjusting the language level. In a company, you will find very different language levels and communication styles, depending on whether you are in a management meeting, at the marketing department's lounge, or among the workers in production (FriederGammGroup, 2022).

Practical tips

- Mirror your negotiation opponent's gestures, posture, and facial expressions. Stay authentic.
- Pay attention to which sensory and value compass the negotiating opponent uses to communicate and perceive; pick him up at this level.

5.5.6 *Appeal to a higher authority*

The "appeal to a higher authority" tactic is characterised by appealing to a higher authority during negotiations, such as management or a supervisor. In this tactic, maximum demands are made to the negotiating opponent under the assumption that they are demanded by the higher authority. In most cases, the negotiating opponent will agree to my demands because they do not want to negotiate directly with their superiors or management. Furthermore, the other side will not question the company's goals as demanded by management.

5.5.7 *Asymmetrical seating arrangement*

A tactic commonly employed, particularly in Asia, involves breaking up the system of a fixed-seating arrangement in which the negotiators face each other. You do not sit opposite the negotiator and irritate him. You can observe the negotiations from the stands yourself. This allows you to assess the mood of the other side and, specifically, break down resistance. If it is recognised that the decision-maker has taken the seating arrangement contrary to the stereotypical structure, this can also lead to irritation and stress for the other side. This circumstance can be used to obtain concessions. It is also conceivable to leave a seat free for the most important decision-makers so that they may be consulted in the event of escalations.

5.5.8 *Shared visions*

Shared visions are also an elementary tactic in negotiations. From a practical point of view, a long-term relationship and partnership make sense in most business relationships, as projects usually last for a longer period of time and can be linked to follow-up orders. In particular, where substituting suppliers or customers is time-consuming and involves high costs, negotiations should aim for a long-term commitment and partnership. Letters of intent or longer-term framework agreements can serve as an ideal tool here, even without an indefinite commitment and complete dependence by the supplier.

References

Abdel-Latif, A. (2015). Nicht verblüffen lassen. Schützen Sie sich vor den zehn dreckigsten Verhandlungsfallen. Available at: https://www.focus.de/ finanzen/experten/adel_abdel-latif/nicht-bluffen-lassen-schuetzen-sie-sich-vor-den-zehn-dreckigsten-verhandlungsfallen_id_4772172.html [Abgerufen am 1 April 2018].

Brost, M. (2017). Verhandlungen. Tipps für eine erfolgreiche Verhandlungsstrategie. Mehr fordern, als man will. Available at: https://www.zeit.de/2017/43/ verhandlungen-politik-training-matthias-schranner [Abgerufen am 11 July 2018].

Fetsch, F. R. (2006). *Verhandeln in Konflikten: Grundlagen – Theorie – Praxis* (German edition). Wiesbaden: Verlag für Sozialwissenschaften.

Fisher, R. and Ury, W. (1981). *Getting to Yes*. London: Penguin Group.

FriederGammGroup (2022). Körpersprache in Verhandlungen geschickt einsetzen. Available at: https://friedergamm.de/koerpersprache-in-verhandlungen/ [Abgerufen am 25 July 2022].

Helmold, M. (2023). *Verhandlungen gewinnen. Konzepte, Methoden und Tools.* Cham: Springer.

Helmold, M., Dathe, T., and Hummel, F. (2019). *Erfolgreiche Verhandlungen. Best-in-Class Empfehlungen für den Verhandlungsdurchbruch.* Wiesbaden: Springer.

Helmold, M., Dathe, T., and Hummel, F. (2022). *Successful Negotiations. Strategies and Tools for the Negotiation Breakthrough.* Cham: Springer.

Pflug, K.-H. (2022). Verhandlungstrick schmeicheln, spiegeln. Available at: http://www.verkaufstricks-verhandlungstricks.de/verhandlungstrick-schmeicheln.html [Abgerufen am 25 July 2022].

Schmitz, R., Spilker, U., and Schmelzer, J. A. (2006). *Strategische Verhandlungsvorbereitung: Ein Leitfaden mit Arbeitshilfen Wie Sie Ihre Ziele in 5 Schritten sicher erreichen.* Wiesbaden: Springer.

Verhandlungstrainings (2022). Verhandlungsstrategien. Available at: https:// www.verhandlungstraining.org/verhandlungsstrategien.html [Abgerufen am 26 July 2022].

Chapter 6

Using the Right Arguments (A-3)

6.1 Argumentation Based on Motives and Interests

Arguing means convincing. Being convinced means more than believing, because conviction is based on evidence (*argumentum*, meaning evidence in Latin). The structure of the negotiation argument and the definition of an argumentation strategy, therefore, represent an important step 3 (A-3) in the A-6 negotiation concept. Arguing correctly means recognising the (possible) interests and motives of the negotiating opponent and placing these at the forefront of your own argument. Although these may not always be clearly recognisable, they can often be determined through astute questioning during a conversation. The more information you get, the more targeted and promising your argument can become. Only when the true motives of the negotiating opponent are clearly recognised is it possible to enter into a measured and goal-oriented argument.

When preparing for an argument, it is advisable to use the arguments of the negotiating opponent for your own purposes and examine them for weaknesses (Brandl, 2012). The opponent's arguments should, therefore, be identified in advance and examined for weaknesses. You should also strengthen your own argument. A strong argument is characterised by the fact that it is well received by the negotiating partner and, ideally, serves their motives. The interests and motives of the other party must always be taken into account. Arguments can be strengthened by highlighting the benefits to the negotiating opponent.

Table 6.1 shows the most important basic rules for the structure and design of powerful arguments.

Table 6.1.   Using the right arguments, strategies, and tactics (A-3).

1.	Take a counter-perspective and look at arguments from the opponent's point of view.
2.	Identify and refute counter arguments and causal relationships between issues.
3.	Use qualitative and quantitative facts and data as a basis for negotiations.
4.	Make a concise formulation of arguments and ensure their prioritisation in the correct order.
5.	Prepare by visualising important issues in international negotiations.

6.2 Order of Arguments

Use your negotiation arguments in the correct order:

- The most important argument: The first argument should be your strongest. It attracts maximum attention and can have a highly positive influence on the further course of the negotiation. Repeat it a few times during the negotiation to anchor it in the subconscious of the negotiating partner.
- The less important argument: 90% of the time, the strongest justification is usually sufficient. If this is not the case, use a second one. The argument can be average, and it may also be doubted by the negotiating partner.
- The second most important argument: If the negotiating partner still has doubts, use your third argument, which justifies your demand with the second strongest force.

6.3 The Negotiation Manuscript as a Common Thread

An important tool for negotiations is the negotiation manuscript (also referred to as a script, screenplay, or manuscript). It serves as an ideal template for negotiating in phase A-4 and helps the negotiator recognise and overcome resistance with the help of scenarios. The script, or negotiation manuscript, as shown in Figure 6.1, is the common thread in every negotiation as part of the A-3 step. The common thread is the basis of the argumentative structure, serving as the basis of one's own negotiations. The manuscript guides the negotiator in a logical and systematic way towards the significant questions in negotiations through the use of

Negotiation Manuscript:	Theme: Negotiator: Date:		1/2
1. Scope & Objectives (What & About What)	What do I want to negotiate? What do I have to negotiate? What can I negotiate? What are the important factors?	What scope/elements do I have to consider? Which interests do I represent?	
Quality Objectives (Q): Qualification, Audits Management Systems Delivery Quality Field Quality Warranty	Cost/Price Objectives (C): Piece Price/Material Cost One-off Costs Warranty Costs Service Costs Payment Terms	Delivery Objectives (D):	
Alpha Objectives (α): Technology Innovation Sustainability Human Resources Marketing	Technologies:	Others:	

2. Personalities (Who)
Alpha: Negotiation Leader (Decision-Maker)
Beta: Supporter, Subject Experts (Influencer)
Gamma: Administrative Supporters (Collaborator)
Omega: Critics (Opponent)
Kappa: Supporter (V-Mann/Undercover Agent)
Delta: Inspector, Watchdog (Guardian)

3. Motives & Interests (Why)	Motives, Interests of Negotiation opponent
4. Strategies and Tactics (How)	Which strategies can I use? Where do I apply pressure? Where do I seek compromise? Where can I enter into cooperation? Where should I possibly give in? Where should I possibly avoid the issue? Where can I use which tactics?

A-6 Negotiation Concept Dr. Marc Helmold

Negotiation Manuscript:	Theme: Negotiator: Date:	2/2
Strategies:	Tactics:	

5. Viewpoint, Stance (Which):	Which viewpoints do I have? Which arguments do I have? How strong are my arguments?
My Arguments:	Counterarguments:

6. Warnings (When)	When should I speak out warnings? At which point I can allow concessions? When should I have a negotiation break or pause?
7. Cultural Aspects (Why, What for)	Which cultural Differences do I have to consider? Which cultural specialities and constraints are given?

A-6 Negotiation Concept Dr. Marc Helmold

Figure 6.1 The A-6 negotiation manuscript.

W-questions. The manuscript of the A-6 negotiation concept contains the following elements:

- Scope (What is being negotiated?)
- Personalities (Who is negotiating?)
- Motives and interests (What is being negotiated about?)
- Strategies and tactics (How is negotiating done?)
- Viewpoints (What positions are there?)
- Warnings (When do I have to give a warning signal?)
- Cultural aspects (Why does my counterpart behave in a certain way?)

Practical tip: If you want to be successful in negotiations, you have to be able to argue well and be prepared for objections. If you weigh these up and present them visually, you are perfectly equipped for both. To be successful in a negotiation, you need one thing above all: good arguments. Before a negotiation, you should therefore consider what arguments you want to use and when. To do this, write down all the arguments and counterarguments that come to mind. From these, you should then select the three or four best ones.

6.4 Focus on Motives and Interests, Not on Positions

The motives and drives of the negotiating partner are of central importance when designing a suitable negotiation structure (Bast, 2022). The decisive factor here is not to concentrate on positions, but rather to focus on motives, wishes, drives, and interests (Schmitz *et al.*, 2006). According to recent motivational research, there are three types of motives:

- Achievement motives
- Sociability motives
- Power motives

Achievement motives are aimed at performance in negotiations. The negotiating opponent wants to achieve a good negotiation result. Those who are positively motivated by achievement want to do something well, better, or the best. These can be certain goals or savings, for example.

The sociability motive is shown by belonging to and the success of a group. In this context, belonging to a group, company, or department is the impetus for the negotiations. Sociability motives can be observed in cultures that display group-oriented behaviour. But this can also be a company in which individual employees act as a group.

The ideal negotiation tool for prioritising motives and associated arguments is the priority matrix. The priority matrix helps to highlight arguments, benefits, advantages and possible counterarguments. The same elements must be considered from the viewpoint of my negotiation opponent and partner (Figure 6.2).

The power motive often manifests itself in the need for negotiators to feel strong and influential during negotiations (McClelland and Boyatzis, 1982). Power-motivated people enjoy demonstrating superiority, be it in an argument or through physical presence (Stangl, 2022). The aim of this power behaviour is to control negotiations, and it is usually only possible by exerting control over individuals (Stangl, 2022).

Figure 6.3 (Working Aid 3) shows the elements that one must concentrate on in order to identify the motives of the negotiating party. To identify the motives of the negotiating opponent, one should therefore take time and pay conscious attention to their statements, arguments, interests, and behaviour. By identifying the motives and interests of the negotiating opponent, the expectations and arguments of the opposing side can usually be predicted well (Helmold *et al.*, 2022).

Priority:	My Arguments: Arguments for the Negotiation Execution	Benefits & Advantages	Possible Counterarguments
1.			
2.			
3.			
4.			
5.			
Priority:	Nego Opponent Arguments: Arguments for the Negotiation Execution	Benefits & Advantages	Possible Counterarguments
1.			
2.			
3.			
4.			
5.			

Figure 6.2 Priority matrix in negotiations.

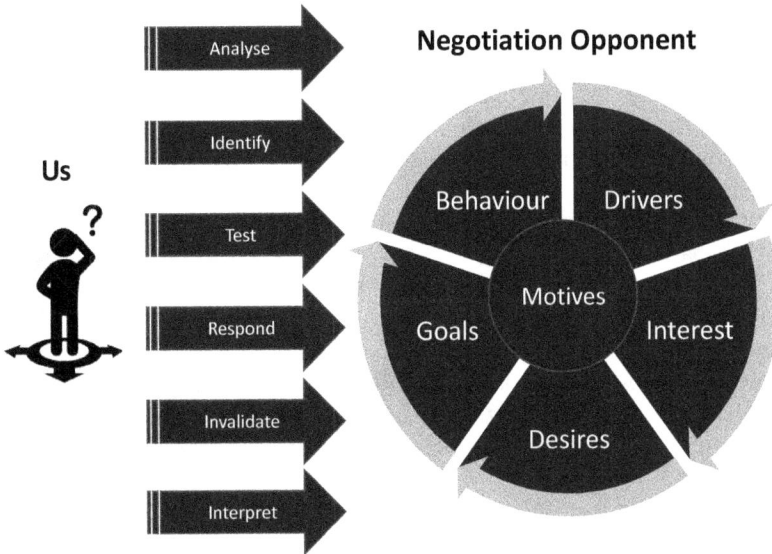

Figure 6.3 Negotiation opponents.

Practical tip: Prepare every negotiation well by assessing and analysing the motives, interests, arguments, and objections. Then, you can use your arguments and stylistic devices precisely to achieve this. And you can show your partner the benefits they can achieve with the negotiation results.

Table 6.2. Recommendations for using the right arguments, facts and assumptions in negotiations.

Recognising the motives of the negotiating party.

Listing the key arguments and objections in the priority matrix.

Identifying the benefits for the negotiating opponent.

Using selected data and facts.

Playing through arguments and counterarguments.

Building a chain of arguments with the formulation of all arguments.

Looking at your own arguments from the perspective of the negotiating partner.

In summary, it can be said that the structured presentation of arguments is a key success factor (Helmold, 2023). This includes the weighting of the arguments and the subsequent prioritisation in the priority matrix. Objections and benefits can also be presented visually here (Table 6.2).

References

Bast, V. (2022). Impulse. Netzwerk und Know-How für Unternehmer. Argumentation in Verhandlungen. Available at: https://www.impulse.de/management/unternehmensfuehrung/argumentation-verhandlung/3559648.html.

Brandl, P. (2012). *30 Minuten Verhandeln: In 30 Minuten wissen Sie mehr!* Offenbach: Gabal.

Helmold, M. (2023). *Verhandlungen gewinnen. Konzepte, Methoden und Tools.* Cham: Springer.

Helmold, M., Dathe, T., and Hummel, F. (2022). *Successful Negotiations. Strategies and Tools for the Negotiation Breakthrough.* Cham: Springer.

McClelland, D. C. and Boyatzis, R. E. (1982). Leadership motive pattern and long-term success in management. *Journal of Applied Psychology*, 67, 737–743.

Schmitz, R., Spilker, U., and Schmelzer, J. A. (2006). *Strategische Verhandlungsvorbereitung: Ein Leitfaden mit Arbeitshilfen Wie Sie Ihre Ziele in 5 Schritten sicher erreichen.* Wiesbaden: Springer.

Stangl, W. (2022). Machtmotiv. *Online Lexikon für Psychologie und Pädagogik.*

Chapter 7

Negotiation Execution (A-4)

The fourth step in the A-6 negotiation concept is the actual negotiation (Figure 7.1). Negotiations must be systematically planned and carried out based on a well-prepared agenda. A negotiation basically takes place in six sub-phases, as shown in Table 7.1 (Erbacher, 2018). Negotiation is the actual game in which both negotiating partners meet.

The major and relevant items for this important phase are shown in Table 7.1.

Figure 7.2 shows the most important aspects in the individual sub-phases. In step 1, negotiation preparation, the agenda, problem description, background, data, information, precedents, legal situation, statistics, preliminary negotiations, information about negotiating partners, taboo topics, positive previous experiences, animosities, and one's own interests, goals, and motives must be coordinated internally. The goal of this phase is thorough preparation, coordination with all departments and interest groups (stakeholders), and the harmonisation of goals and demands within one's own negotiating side (O'brien, 2016). The negotiation script and additional tools can ideally be used for this. The respective goals and sub-goals must also be categorised and weighted in a priority matrix. Scenarios can also be presented in the event that agreement cannot be reached on sub-goals. In addition to the negotiation points, the roles must be distributed, e.g., negotiator, moderator, use of external consultants, observer, and secretary. It is also advisable to discuss tactics and strategies, for example, the allocation of roles such as "good cop and bad cop".

Step 2 involves determining the negotiation room and seating arrangement. In Western countries, less attention is paid to the selection of the

Figure 7.1.   Negotiation execution.

Table 7.1.   Execution steps (A-4).

1.	Negotiation preparation
2.	Room allocation and seating arrangement
3.	Greetings and introductions
4.	Main part of the negotiation
5.	End and summary
6.	Farewell and dispersal

meeting room and its location than in Asian or Arab countries. In addition to your own seating arrangement, you can also tactically influence the seating arrangements of the other side by trying to position influencers on their side.

Step 3 focuses on the greeting. This phase can last several minutes, especially in an international environment. All participants should have their business cards within reach to introduce themselves. In countries where there is a strong hierarchy, paying attention to one's position and status is an important element of an introduction.

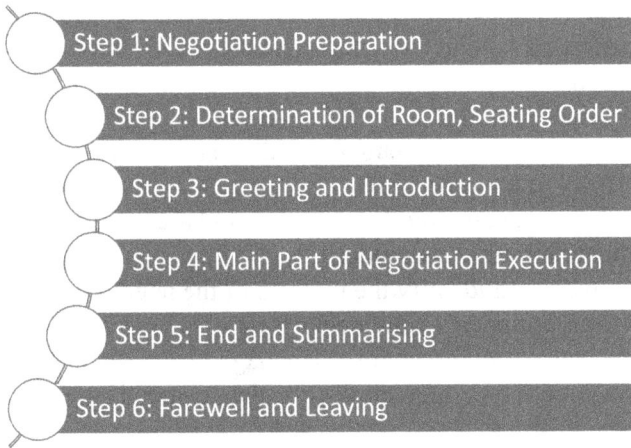

Figure 7.2. Sub-phases of the A-4 phase: negotiation execution.

Step 4 is the actual core negotiation. This part should be clearly structured by an agenda and run systematically.

After all negotiation points have been discussed, the results and agreements should be summarised in step 5. The protocol should be signed by both parties and should also highlight differences in opinion and disagreements (Helmold, 2018, 2023).

The final, sixth step is the farewell. In Asian countries, the negotiating party may stay outside the building and wave goodbye until they are out of sight.

Practical tip: Stick to the order and determine the pace of the negotiations. Take the driver's seat in terms of agenda, pace, and negotiation execution. While doing this, be polite and use analytical listening techniques.

7.1 Recommendations for Successful Negotiation

Negotiation is the analytical and systematic attempt to use strategic, tactical, and methodical behaviour to achieve previously set negotiation goals through negotiation and interaction with the negotiating opponent (Rock, 2018; Helmold, 2023). Certain criteria and rules must be observed for the actual negotiation (Schranner, 2015). The A-6 concept recommends the following rules of conduct for negotiations, which have proven themselves in practice:

- Focus your argument on a target corridor and not on a static goal.
- Show respect to the other side.
- Pay attention to intercultural aspects in all phases of the negotiation.
- Show attention to the other side.
- Listen actively and identify the motives of the negotiating partner.
- Express your arguments convincingly.
- Convince with slightly emotional language.
- Let the negotiation partner speak first, then respond.
- If you have nothing to say, don't speak.
- Do not immediately respond to statements from the negotiating opponent.
- State your strongest argument first.
- Try to understand and speak the language of your negotiating partner.
- Prioritise your arguments.
- Consider the arguments from the other side's point of view.
- Emphasise the importance of your arguments, not their correctness.
- Refute the arguments of the other side.
- Focus on weak points in the arguments of the negotiating side.
- Focus on the negotiation partner's weakest argument.
- Only make concessions where it is useful.
- Demand something in return for concessions.

Practical tip: The first argument should be your strongest. It attracts maximum attention and can have a very positive influence on the further course of the negotiation. Repeat it a few times during the negotiation to anchor it in the negotiation partner's subconscious. Ninety percent of the time, the strongest justification is sufficient.

7.2 The Power of the Negotiation Location

The negotiation location, room design, and seating arrangement have an important influence on the climate of negotiations. The design of the room layout as well as the external conditions, such as seating arrangement,

arrangement of chairs, lighting conditions, climatic conditions, drinks or not, and catering or not, can have a lasting negative or positive impact on the negotiations. By choosing the right room size, climatic conditions, lighting conditions, drinks, or snacks, you can create a basic positive attitude and show the negotiating partner that you value good relationships and a harmonious atmosphere. In contrast to a comfortable atmosphere, it is possible to create an uncomfortable negotiating climate by using the so-called "dirty tricks", such as using a room that is too small, too cold, or too hot (O'brien, 2016). The negotiation partner feels uncomfortable and wants nothing more than to leave the negotiating location. This leads him to make rash concessions.

Practical tip: The golden rule is that the negotiating partner should always sit near the door. This leads to a comfortable feeling, as theoretically they can leave the room at any time. If you want the negotiating partner to feel uncomfortable, you can change this rule and specify a mixed seating arrangement (e.g., with name tags) or a seat by the window.

7.3 Questioning Techniques in Negotiations

7.3.1 *Use and application of questioning techniques*

Questioning techniques involve the use of targeted, tactical questions to guide a focused conversation. Questions are not asked merely to obtain answers or clarify an acute situation. They are used to guide the conversation and create a suitable atmosphere for it (Grochowiak and Heiligtag, 2002). Questions also indicate interest in a matter, a topic, or a person, i.e., to express emotional involvement (Helmold *et al.*, 2022). Every person who is asked to answer a question about decision-making feels honoured. Questions lead to further advancement in communication. Unconsciously, those being asked always react as the communication "ball" is passed to them (Patrzek, 2017). That is why questioning techniques are a proven way to implement your own tactical calculations in communication.

7.3.2 *Open questions*

Your conversation partner can answer open questions in a number of ways. These questions open up the conversation and serve to obtain important information from the negotiating partner. Open questions are intended to lure the negotiation partner out of their shell. Examples of open questions in negotiations are described in Table 7.2. They are usually used at the beginning of negotiations.

7.3.3 Closed questions

Closed questions are characterised by the fact that there are only two possible answers: affirmation (yes) or negation (no). Closed questions usually have a manipulative effect on the negotiating partner and can be used in such a way that the negotiation partner has to answer the question with a "yes" or "no", as shown in Table 7.3. This questioning technique can also be used to obtain specific information.

7.3.4 Alternative questions

There are two different options for alternative questions (Table 7.4). This questioning technique is also used for manipulation and can distract the

Table 7.2.   Open questions: examples.

What important criteria do you have in mind for the deal?
What price do you want so that we can close the deal?
What other competitors are there in the tender?
When do you intend to award the contract?
What criteria are important to you when manufacturing the product so that we can meet your requirements?

Table 7.3.   Closed questions.

Do you want these features?
Is quality important to you?
Are you the decision-maker for the project?
Do you need a good manufacturer for the product?
Do you want to place the order today?
Is Mr. Meier the responsible decision-maker for the order?

negotiation partner, e.g., "Would you like to buy product A or product B?" Alternative questions make the opposing negotiation side focus on two of the alternatives we want, so that other options are excluded.

7.3.5 Leading questions

Leading questions, such as those listed in Table 7.5, are characterised by the fact that the negotiating partner only has to agree to a specific proposal. With leading questions, negotiation experts succeed in subtly steering and manipulating the other side towards their own direction. It is crucial that this questioning technique be used only in moderation so that the negotiation partner does not feel too manipulated.

7.3.6 Stimulating and motivating questions

Stimulating and motivating questions are used to create a positive mood. Stimulating questions are often used in an international context in the form of flattery. Examples are: "How do you know our country so well?" or "Why do you know our local customs and language so well?" Stimulating questions should be asked with the help of subliminal and

Table 7.4. Alternative questions.

Do you want these or those features?
Is quality or price more important to you?
Do you want to award the contract today or tomorrow?
Are you or Mr. Meier the decision-maker for the project?
Do you want to buy the red or blue car?

Table 7.5. Leading questions.

You certainly think quality is more important than just price?
You also think it is important that we can significantly increase your potential with this service?
You also want a long-term partnership?
You certainly want to leave the business with the best result?
You certainly want this feature?

subtle praise in order to put the negotiating partner in a positive mood. Especially with egocentric and alpha individuals, it is advisable to incorporate stimulating questions at intervals in order to appeal to their egos. Table 7.6 shows examples of stimulating and motivating questions.

7.3.7 Rhetorical questions

Rhetorical questions, as shown in Table 7.7, target the emotional needs of the negotiation partners and stimulate them to think and participate. The other side is encouraged to identify their own arguments and to view suggestions as positive. The credibility of the suggestion is also significantly increased by adding pictorial or metaphorical examples. This questioning technique, therefore, is a key to reaching out to the emotional needs of negotiation partners and thus generating a high level of motivation. According to studies, 80% of our purchasing decisions are made on an emotional level.

7.3.8 Confirmation questions

Confirmation questions signal a connection and an emotional closeness to the negotiating partner. These demonstrate to the negotiation partner that their fears, worries, and needs are understood through active listening. Confirmation questions, also called mirroring questions, can be effectively used to create a personal bond with the negotiation partner.

Table 7.6.   Stimulation and motivation questions.

Are you responsible for this great organisation?

Did you ensure that the negotiation results were implemented immediately and in a first-class manner?

Did you ensure that the website was professional?

Did you ensure that the exhibition was great?

Did you choose the great restaurant?

Table 7.7.   Rhetorical questions.

Can you imagine how we can successfully expand our long-term partnership?

Can you imagine how efficient your business processes are when you use our product?

Do you have any idea how satisfied your customers are when they use our product?

Table 7.8. Confirmation questions.

Am I right in assuming that your purchase decision is based on the TCO principle and includes all costs?

If I have understood you correctly, you want a car with low consumption so that the subsequent costs for you are as low and predictable as possible?

Do I understand you correctly that you want to buy the best quality product?

If I understand you correctly, the goods should be available the next day because, after all, your customers expect you to be able to pick up products within 24 hours?

Table 7.9. Indirect questions.

Intended Information	Indirect Question
Prospects of winning the contract	I assume that there are two competitors who can win the contract?
Degree of internationalisation of the supplier and experience with foreign customers	I think that you already have numerous international clients?
Target price range and value of the total budget for the current project	In the last big project you had a budget of EUR 1 million?

Confirmation questions will be answered by the other party with a clear confirmation ("Yes, that's right!"). Table 7.8 shows examples of confirmation questions.

7.3.9 Indirect questions

The use of indirect questions is recommended when direct questions are inappropriate. In order to obtain relevant and useful information, the question is ostensibly about another topic. However, this question is formulated in such a way that the answer provides information about the actual question. Table 7.9 shows examples of indirect questions.

7.4 Discussion and Negotiator Types

In addition to using questioning techniques, it is useful to respond to personality types in a meaningful and effective manner. Table 7.10 shows different discussion types and the recommended behaviour for each. A mixture or combination of discussion types is often encountered in practice.

Table 7.10. Negotiation and discussion types.

Negotiation Type	Description for Negotiation	Recommended Style and Behaviour
The experienced one	Experienced and routine	Rely on experience and appeal
The clever one		Appeal to the ego with stimulating questions
The argumentative one	Arrogant and dominant	Stay objective and calm; encourage constructive behaviour
The exalted one	Destructive	Give few direct answers; let opponents speak
The omniscient one	Criticism	Ask closed questions
The talkative one	Waiting to trick someone	Interrupt tactfully; agree on speaking times
The lazy one	Knows everything better than the others	Ask directly for opinions; enable experiences of success
The blocker	Talks for the sake of talking	Stay objective; address directly; break off negotiations; exclude from negotiations
The reserved one	Uninterested and bored	Involve and ask easy and closed questions

Practical tip: Use questioning techniques to break through negotiations. Show your opponent that you are leading the negotiations. Use different question types based on the situation. Understand which discussion type you are negotiating with, and select your responding style.

References

Erbacher, C. E. (2018). *Grundzüge der Verhandlungsvorbereitung.* Zürich: VDF.
Grochowiak, K. and Heiligtag, S. (2002). *Die Magie des Fragens.* Paderborn: Junfermann.
Helmold, M. (2023). *Verhandlungen gewinnen. Konzepte, Methoden und Tools.* Cham: Springer.
Helmold, M., Dathe, T., and Hummel, F. (2022). *Successful Negotiations. Strategies and Tools for the Negotiation Breakthrough.* Cham: Springer.

O'Brien, J. (2016). *Negotiations for Procurement Professionals*, 2nd edn. Croyden: Kogan Page.

Patrzek, A. (2017). *Systemisches Fragen: Professionelle Fragetechnik für Führungskräfte, Berater und Coaches*, 2. Auflage. Wiesbaden: Springer.

Rock, H. (2018). *Field Guide für Verhandlungsführer: Drei Basisstrategien für erfolgreiche Verhandlungen und Konfliktlösungen. Essentials.* Wiesbaden: Springer.

Schranner, M. (2015). 7 Prinzipien für erfolgreiches Verhandeln. [Abgerufen am 20 March 2018].

Chapter 8

Recognising and Breaking Resistance (A-5)

8.1 Opposing Positions and Resistance

Within the accomplishment and amplification of the negotiation, it is important to ascertain resistance and attack counterarguments and resistance (A-5; Figure 8.1).

Resistance in negotiations and counterarguments are normal elements in negotiations. Resistance to change, or agreement on negotiation proposals, is a systematic or open reluctance or refusal for people to adapt to change. The opposition can range from expressing their resistance publicly to unknowingly resisting change through micro-resistance, language, or general actions. Overcoming resistance in negotiations is about striking the right balance between empathy and strategy. Figure 8.2 shows the resistance–concerns matrix.

The matrix shows factual issues in relation to personal concerns. Resistance fighters have strong, factual, and personal concerns. As this group is not willing to change for the better, it is advisable to either get rid of them or to minimise factual or personal concerns.

- Stoppers have high personal concerns and low, if any, factual concerns. Here, it is recommended to build up a relationship.
- Sceptics have factual concerns and can be convinced with fact-based arguments.
- Supporters can be utilised, as their personal and factual concerns are very low.

- Resistance fighters are toxic and may sabotage the negotiation or proposals. It is important to get rid of them during negotiations.

Figure 8.1. A-5: handling resistance and counterarguments.

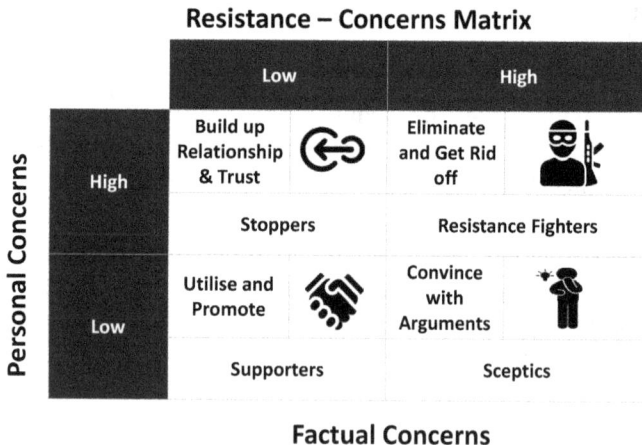

Figure 8.2. Resistance–concerns matrix.

Opposing negotiating positions and resistance are omnipresent in negotiations. Resistance during negotiations is defined as rejection, oppositional action, or refusal in relation to certain proposals or negotiation positions. Resistance usually arises from opposing opinions, interests, and motives. It is characterised in negotiations by the fact that it is exercised either consciously or unconsciously by negotiating opponents. Resistance in negotiations occurs in a wide variety of forms, verbal or non-verbal, which in most cases people involved are not aware of. In negotiations, resistance is expressed through language (verbal) or through gestures or facial expressions (non-verbal, i.e., behaviour or facial expressions). The decisive factor in breaking resistance is recognising rejections or contrary positions by the negotiating opponent and identifying their motives to refute or overcome resistance (Helmold *et al.*, 2022). There are many reasons for resistance (Zielke, 2021), as follows:

- fears of the negotiating counterpart when proposals are viewed as threatening;
- a lack of mandates or restrictions in individual negotiating positions;
- resistance from interest groups of the negotiating party;
- self-interests of the negotiating party;
- tactical considerations of the other side if other negotiating points are to be won in this way;
- revenge or retaliation if negotiating opponents want to thwart plans;
- unfinished business from previous negotiations;
- previous experiences or experiences from other negotiations.

8.2 Open Resistance

Open resistance is characterised by the fact that it is consciously exercised by the negotiating opponents and that they also associate goals with it. Open resistance is relatively easy to recognise because the characteristics and behaviours are openly evident:

- open contradiction (example: "I disagree..."),
- open rejection (example: "I cannot agree with your suggestion..."),
- open intervention (example: "I cannot agree with your suggestion. I therefore suggest that..."),
- rejection through obvious head shaking,
- rejection through gestures with the arms or index finger.

Open resistance usually has a rational cause that can be discussed with those affected, and parties have an interest in overcoming it. This form of resistance is usually constructive; thus, it is possible to deal with open resistance (Helmold, 2023). Breaking resistance or refuting and mitigating it with fact-based arguments can be a suitable strategy here (Helmold & Terry, 2016). This allows the energy that the resisting people have invested in their resistance to be channelled towards achieving the negotiation goal.

8.3 Hidden and Covert Resistance

Dealing with covert or latent resistance is much more difficult. With this form of resistance, those who are resisting usually have no interest in being recognised (Hilsenbeck, 2004). For personal or tactical reasons, they act from the background or from the second row. Their interests are usually of a destructive nature, i.e., they want to prevent something without being recognised as the perpetrators. Paradoxically, in many cases, those resisting may not be aware of their resistance. This makes dealing with this form of resistance even more difficult (Volk, 2018). If the covert resistance is not recognised in time, the entire negotiation result may be at stake. Hidden resistance in negotiations can manifest itself in the following ways:

- comments and statements with qualifications (example: "I understand your point of view, but..."),
- the absence of important decision-makers (alpha types) or influential people (beta types),
- the late arrival of important decision-makers (alpha types) or influential people (beta types) to negotiations,
- the permanent postponement of negotiations due to alleged scheduling difficulties,
- non-verbal signals of resistance such as mental absence or disinterest,
- the demand for perfect solutions,
- the demand that the negotiating opponent moves first,
- the extensive and lengthy consideration and discussion of relatively unimportant special cases,
- agreeing in principle while simultaneously expressing reservations that are to be clarified later.

8.4 Dealing with Resistance

Resistance must be recognised in negotiations, and it is also crucial to question the underlying motives of the resistance. In cases where there is open and rational resistance, counterarguments and reformulating one's own goals can help weaken this resistance and achieve negotiation results. In cases where issues are not pivotal to negotiations, it is possible to disregard resistance and either respond to the demands of the negotiating opponent or address them at a later point in time. If the resistance cannot be resolved, which applies to key points of the negotiations, the negotiations are likely to be unsuccessful. Unconscious or hidden resistance is more difficult to recognise:

1. Recognise resistance.
2. Assess resistance.
3. Refute resistance.
4. Break resistance.

It is advisable to listen to the other side and understand their motives as soon as you recognise resistance (Volk, 2018). A change of location or a

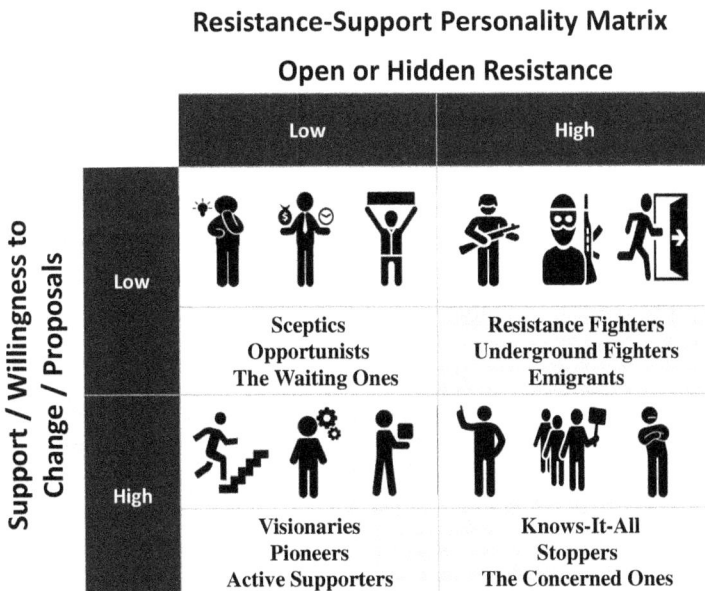

Figure 8.3. Resistance–support matrix.

Table 8.1.   Fighting resistance and counterarguments.

Recognise and understand resistance.

Resistance can also be broken through warnings.

Break resistance through fact-based arguments.

Give in and make concessions where your priorities do not lie.

Change the location of negotiations when faced with resistance.

Distractions can be helpful when faced with resistance.

discussion over lunch or dinner may lead the resistant party to open up and articulate their motives and reasons for the resistance directly or indirectly.

The resistance–support personality matrix shows the personalities in relation to their willingness to change and level of open resistance (Figure 8.3).

The group of people who show willingness to embrace change and provide support in combination with a low resistance consists of visionaries, pioneers, or active supporters (Helmold, 2023). This group will be in favour of ongoing changes and proposals.

Table 8.1 shows the recommendations for fighting and overcoming resistance and counterarguments.

Visionaries

Visionaries are ahead of their future and carry a vision with them. Lean management and the transformation to a lean, future-oriented and innovative company serve as the driving forces for visionaries and missionaries. The lean company thus describes a performance-oriented, excellent, efficient, and constantly self-optimising organisation in which all processes are geared towards the customer in order to eliminate non-value-adding activities. Visionaries and missionaries can inspire others with their ideas, values, and guiding principles.

Pioneers

Pioneers are trailblazers and represent an important group in the transformation towards lean management. Pioneers are usually specialists in lean management who can lead and implement lean management projects thanks to their experience. Pioneers are also used for training. They have a very high willingness to change and drive it forward.

Active supporters

Active supporters are employees who believe in the transformation to a lean company. Supporters are helpful in the transformation and help to promote motivation. They are positively open to change and actively participate in projects.

On the contrary, negotiators or people with high resistance and low willingness to change are called resistance fighters, underground fighters, or emigrants.

Open resistance fighters

Open resistance is characterised by the fact that it is consciously exercised by those who resist and that they also associate a goal with it. In addition, those who exercise resistance deliberately want their resistance to be perceived as such and to be attributed to them. They usually do this from a position to which they themselves attribute a relative amount of power. This open resistance, therefore, has the advantage that it can be the subject of supplier management and processing; the cards are, so to speak, on the table. Forms of open resistance can be as follows:

- open contradiction,
- open criticism,
- frequent complaints,
- open interventions or activities that are directed against the planned project.

This open resistance is usually based on rational causes that can be discussed with those affected and that all those involved have an interest in overcoming it. This form of resistance is usually constructive, so that it is possible to deal with open resistance. This allows the energy that the resistant people have invested in their resistance to be channelled towards achieving the project goals, or, to put it simply, the headwind becomes the tailwind.

Underground fighters

Underground fighters are those who harbour reservations and do not approve of the change and, therefore, do not support it. Underground fighters operate in secrecy, and they sabotage changes. Underground fighters hinder the transformation to lean management through hidden or latent resistance. In this context, the employee who is resisting usually has no interest in being recognised. They operate in secret for personal or tactical reasons. Their interests are usually of a destructive nature, i.e., they want to prevent something without being recognised as the cause. Paradoxically, in many cases, those resisting may not be aware of their resistance.

This makes dealing with this form of resistance even more difficult. If the hidden resistance is not recognised in time, ticking time bombs can be easily created; their destructive power increases over time, potentially leading to project failure. Symptoms and manifestations of hidden resistance can be observed frequently and in many different forms during practical project work, including the following:

- a lack of motivation at work;
- increasing absences that cannot be specifically explained or for spurious reasons, even to the point of increasing sickness rates;
- acting less knowledgeable than one actually is;
- increasing questions about unimportant topics;
- repeatedly questioning decisions that have already been made;
- avoiding specific requests to do or not do something;
- increasing re-delegation of tasks that have already been accepted;
- sitting out problems;
- hectic actionism in unimportant areas;
- demanding maximum involvement of unimportant stakeholders;
- silence in places where communication would be called for;
- abstaining from important meetings or sending representatives who do not have the authority to make decisions;
- demanding perfect solutions;
- demanding that others move first;
- extensive consideration and discussion of special cases;
- general agreement while simultaneously registering reservations that will be clarified later.

Hidden or latent resistance can only be clearly diagnosed in particularly pronounced cases, as individual symptoms and signals may also have other causes.

Emigrants

Emigrants are people who are critical of change and remove themselves from the group. These people are often associated with "internal resignation", or self-abandonment. The dissatisfaction leads to this group of people deciding to leave the company. In the case of emigrants, it is therefore advisable to let them go immediately (Helmold, 2023). In particular, by hiring motivated individuals who are positive about change, a "breath of fresh air" can be created that significantly supports the change.

People or negotiators who show low willingness to change or accept with low resistance usually wait for greater clarity and transparency. This group consists of sceptics, opportunists, and the waiting ones.

Sceptics

Sceptics have hidden or open concerns about the negotiation proposal or project. This group is inclined to question or doubt accepted opinions (Helmold, 2023). Sceptics should be taken seriously. It is important to listen to the concerns and to share facts from reputable and widely accepted sources. Quantifiable data can help to quash misperceptions and bolster your talking points.

Opportunists

Opportunists are employees and individuals who act expediently to adapt to situations and take advantage of them. Opportunism is often described in political and social terms as behaviour without principles or character. Although these people are not convinced of the change, they support the change process and work on projects.

The waiting ones

Wait-and-see people are employees who have not yet fully decided whether they want to go along with the changes or hinder them. This personality group doubts whether the change will bring advantages or disadvantages on the surface. Wait-and-see people must be convinced by management and change managers and must feel inspired about the change (Helmold, 2022).

People with high resistance and high support are considered to be know-it-alls, stoppers, or concerned once.

Know-it-alls

The know-it-alls have a high motivation for changes and proposals. They want to sit in the driver's seat. It is recommended to use proper tact, feeling, and assertiveness. It can be helpful to set strict boundaries to show that resistance must be eliminated.

Stoppers

Stoppers might be slowing down the project and the proposals made. Stoppers need to be confronted with their actions and the outcomes of their resistance. Stoppers must have clear boundaries, too.

Concerned ones
The concerns have reasons to show resistance. It can be helpful to be mindful, pause, and then consider a thoughtful, compassionate response.

8.5 Approaching and Defending against Counterarguments

Counterarguments from negotiating partners can be refuted by facts. If their demands do not correspond to your own priorities, you can make concessions here in order to be able to demand concessions from the other side in significant aspects. In addition, when defending against and refuting counterarguments, your own arguments can become even clearer by using certain conjunctions or linguistic formulations and connecting them to both the counterarguments and your own arguments, for example:

- You are right on certain points, but on closer inspection...
- I understand your argument; nevertheless,...
- I have understood your point of view; however,...
- Even if you are of the opinion that..., I am still of the opinion...
- Of course it is true that..., but...
- It is certainly correct...; nevertheless, I think...
- I admit that..., but in my opinion...
- It is true that...; however,...

In addition to defending against counterarguments by identifying weaknesses in the argument, a warning can be a useful tool for defending against counterarguments. Warnings are fact-based, rational signals and arguments for rejecting a negotiating counterpart's positions, which are usually exaggerated or unacceptable, instead of issuing threats.

8.6 Positive and Negative Negotiation to Ward Off Resistance

The type of negotiation must be applied situationally and flexibly within Dr. Marc Helmold's negotiation concept. Negotiation can be consciously implemented either positively or negatively. Table 8.2 shows examples of both positive and negative types of negotiations, which are of central

Table 8.2.   Positive and negative negotiations.

Negotiation Style	Topic	Example
Positive negotiation	Growth opportunities	Do you want to be our prime partner for new projects…? There are many new projects and customers coming.
Positive negotiation	Innovations	What are you doing for being innovative…? We want to work with the most innovative partner.
Positive negotiation	The pole position	Do you want to be with us in the pole position…? You are our prime partner. We can be successful in our collaboration.
Negative negotiation	Difficult times	How are you helping us to survive in difficult times…? Competition is getting stronger. Survival in the market is difficult. This requires cuts everywhere.
Negative negotiation	Change of environment	What are you doing to stay in the market…? The environment and macro parameters changed significantly.
Negative negotiation	Significant market changes	What are you doing to show that you are competitive…? We are confronted with a new market situation. In order to maintain competitiveness, we must agree on…

importance in step A-5. The topics help the reader in applying them practically within respective negotiation situations.

8.7   Show Power through Competence

Formal and informal power are important elements in negotiations (Wilkes, 2016). The formally specified position-based power is based mainly on hierarchical structures and hierarchy levels, which are usually shown in an organisational chart, while informal power is not necessarily based on this basis. The formal organisational structure is the result of a structured and systematic hierarchy that management considers appropriate. Basic elements of the organisational structure consist of positions categorised into groups and departments as subsystems, along with their respective reporting channels. The cooperation between the subsystems is determined by the process organisation that regulates the work processes. The organisational chart is a graphic representation of the organisational structure that shows communication channels and processes. In addition to formal power, there are power structures that are not immediately visible and are based on informal circumstances. Often, people are granted special authority by the members of a group because of their personal characteristics (e.g., high level of professional competence, long-term collaboration, and extensive experience). An informal leader can have an integrating and stabilising effect. However, conflicts can also arise with the superior (the formal leader).

8.8   Informal Power and Organisational Structures

In business and negotiation practice, however, it is often found that the officially defined structure is usually not identical to the actual structure (Grochowiak, 2015). In addition to the formal company organisation, informal phenomena arise as a result of unplanned human behaviour. The reason for this is the individual needs and ideas of the employees. They manifest themselves in the following informal types:

- interest groups,
- communication,
- processes,
- organisational structures,
- norms,
- leaders.

If the formal and informal power structures are understood, they form the starting point for recognising and overcoming resistance. Formal power structures consist of both the organisational structure and processes of the organisation. Informal power structures are more likely to arise from charismatic leaders and their experience, knowledge, or membership in a group. Informal leaders can be identified by an undercover agent and used to achieve their own goals and interests. If the organisational

Table 8.3.   Recommendations for step A-5.

Understanding formal and informal power structures.

Formal power structures: recognising the organisational structure and reporting lines by understanding the organisational structure and process organisation (organisational charts and process descriptions).

Informal power structures: using the liaison person (undercover agent) to understand power relationships (formal and informal).

Recognising formal leaders and those who influence them.

Understanding informal leaders, norms, and processes.

Identifying potential critics and possibly using their arguments for your own purposes.

Warn, don't threaten – put warnings into action if the negotiating opponent does not give up resistance.

Using techniques of positive and negative negotiation.

structure and processes are known, negotiation success can be achieved through positive or negative negotiations. If warnings from the other side are not taken seriously, the warning should always be put into action. Table 8.3 shows the final recommendations for step A-5 in Dr. Marc Helmold's negotiation concept.

> **Practical tip:** Analyse your negotiation opponents in terms of willingness to support/change or to resist. Use positive and negative negotiation tactics. Show power and competency and lead the negotiations.

References

Helmold, M. (2023). *Verhandlungen gewinnen. Konzepte, Methoden und Tools.* Cham: Springer.

Helmold, M. and Terry, B. (2016). *Lieferantenmanagement 2030.* Wiesbaden: Springer Gabler.

Helmold, M., Dathe, T., and Hummel, F. (2022). *Successful Negotiations. Strategies and Tools for the Negotiation Breakthrough.* Cham: Springer.

Volk, H. (2018). Emotionale Dynamik eines Gespräches verstehen. Was den alltäglichen Wortwechsel entgleiten lässt. *Beschaffung aktuell*, 06.2018, 70–71.

Wilkes, K. (2016). Was bewegt Matthias Schranner? Zehn Millionen mehr, bitte! Available at: https://www.zeit.de/2016/22/matthias-schranner-verhandlungs-fuehrer-regierung-geiselnahme [Abgerufen am 17 May 2018].

Zielke, C. (2021). *Kritiker überzeugen: Wirksame Strategien für Verhandlungen, Gespräche und Konflikte* (Haufe Fachbuch). München: Haufe.

Chapter 9

Agreement and End of Negotiations (A-6)

9.1 Recording and Ratification of the Agreements

A-6 (Figure 9.1) is the last step in Dr. Marc Helmold's negotiation concept, and it is of central importance in the design of the contract. Once an agreement has been reached, both negotiating parties should record all important points in writing in a protocol and countersign them as confirmation. It is also advisable to draw up an action plan, outlining responsibilities and deadlines, so that both negotiating parties can ascertain if the agreed-upon activities are being adhered to. Concretising the negotiation results is a fundamental step to avoid intentional or unintentional misinterpretations (Helmold *et al.,* 2022). It is advisable to summarise all results and agreements verbally at the end of the negotiations. Ideally, after negotiations, the draft of the contract should already be completed, which includes key points and milestones. Mutual stocktaking can also be carried out, which is then confirmed by the legal department. When formulating agreements, care must be taken to ensure that no or few advance payments have to be made. In addition, it is appropriate to hold a celebration to officially ratify the contracts during international negotiations. This can be used ideally for marketing purposes and as a motivator within the company in the presence of customers, employees, and other interest groups. Asian companies also often use these occasions to issue press releases. In addition to the celebrations, the negotiators should thank the negotiating team and thereby recognise them.

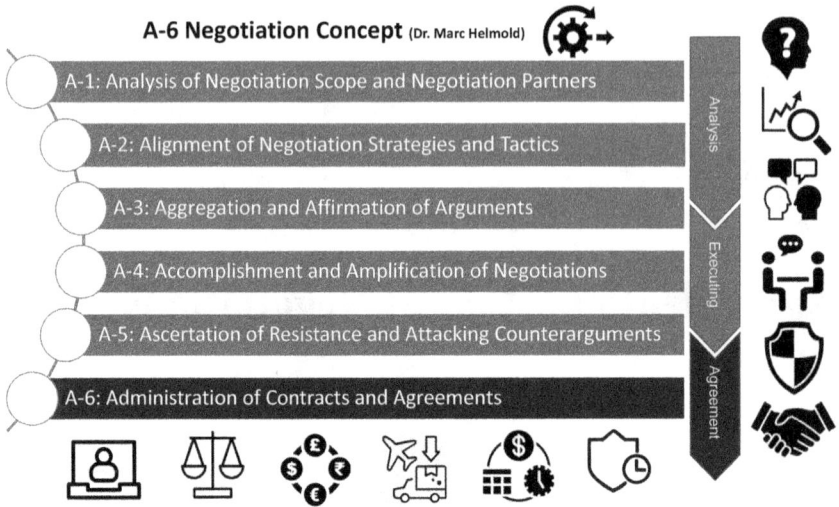

Figure 9.1.   Agreement in negotiations.

9.2 Design of the Agreements and Content of (International) Contracts

9.2.1 *Central elements in international legal transactions*

Due to the increasing international nature of commercial transactions through sales or procurement, international legal transactions are also becoming more important. International legal transactions contain certain special features that must be considered when ratifying contracts. The following points should be taken into account in international negotiations and agreements:

- place of jurisdiction;
- choice of law, such as the UN Convention on Contracts for the International Sale of Goods;
- place of performance, delivery dates, and Incoterms 2020;
- warranty and guarantees;
- interest, and default interest;
- payment transactions, currency, and choice of bank.

9.2.2 Place of jurisdiction

The jurisdiction of courts is the question of which court must exercise jurisdiction in an individual case; in this sense, it refers to the court with local, material, and functional jurisdiction. Determining the contractual place of jurisdiction means choosing the court that should hear any disputes between the parties. Jurisdiction is usually of crucial importance when there are differences between the parties, particularly when one of the two (or sometimes both) parties considers their rights to have been violated and wants to restore them. When concluding the contract, the parties are entitled to determine the place of jurisdiction of their own choosing. However, the parties may refrain from traditional jurisdiction in their contract and designate either a state or commercial court as the forum to resolve their disputes.

9.2.3 UN Convention on Contracts for the International Sale of Goods

In the case of international sales contracts, the question of the applicability of the UN Convention on Contracts for the International Sale of Goods, which is also known as the Vienna Convention on Contracts for the International Sale of Goods and is based on the "United Nations Convention on Contracts for the International Sale of Goods" of 11 April 1980 (CISG), always arises in commercial sales (IHK Berlin, 2018). The geographical scope of application of the UN Convention on Contracts for the International Sale of Goods is established according to Article 1 CISG when a sales contract is concluded between contracting parties whose branches are located in different states, provided that each is a contracting state to the CISG, or their international private law declares the CISG to be applicable. The nationalities of the contracting parties, their merchant status, and whether the contract pertains to commercial or civil law are irrelevant. In addition, the contracting parties can contractually agree upon the applicability of the CISG. In factual terms, the UN Convention on Contracts for the International Sale of Goods applies if the subject of the contract is the purchase of goods. "Goods", within the meaning of the UN Convention on Contracts for the International Sale of Goods, refer to merely movable objects. Sales contracts for land and rights are therefore not covered by the UN Convention on Contracts for the International Sale of Goods. In addition, according to Article 2 CISG, the UN Convention on Contracts for the International Sale of Goods does not apply to sales contracts for securities and means of payment, watercraft, and aircraft, nor to auctions, foreclosures, or other legal measures. Furthermore, the UN Convention on Contracts for the International Sale of Goods does not apply to cross-border contracts for the purchase of goods intended for personal use. Finally, the UN Convention on Contracts for the International Sale of Goods does not apply to contracts in which the focus is not on the transfer of possession and ownership of an item for consideration but rather on the execution of work or other services. An example of this is the preparation of an expert opinion, which may ultimately be submitted in written form; however, the focus is actually on intellectual performance (IHK Berlin, 2018). The UN Convention on Contracts for the International Sale of Goods does not comprehensively regulate the legal aspects of a sales contract. For example, it contains no provisions regarding the limitation of claims or producer liability. In these areas, the applicable national law remains decisive.

9.2.4 *Place of performance and Incoterms 2020*

The International Chamber of Commerce (ICC) in Paris has been publishing "International Rules for the Interpretation of Commercial Contract Terms" since 1936; they are commonly referred to as International Commercial Terms, or Incoterms. Since then, the Incoterms have been repeatedly adapted to changing trade practices, most recently in autumn 2020 (Helmold *et al.*, 2022). The Incoterms are globally recognised, uniform contract and delivery terms that enable the parties to a sales contract to carry out standardised processing in international and national trade. The Incoterms determine the distribution of costs, the distribution of risks, and the duty of care between the contracting parties. The importance of the Incoterms rules lies in the clarity of the mutual obligations gained through their use (IHK Berlin, 2025). With the help of the Incoterms, misunderstandings and costly disputes can be prevented, thus reducing the risk of legal complications for both contracting parties. Legal problems such as the conclusion of a contract, the transfer of ownership, the processing of payments, and dealing with the legal consequences of breaching a contract are not regulated. The decisive factor here is either the provisions of the sales contract or those of the underlying law. Table 9.1 provides a brief

Table 9.1. Incoterms 2020.

EXW	Ex Works
FCA	Free Carrier
FAS	Free Alongside Ship
FOB	Free on Board
CFR	Cost and Freight
CIF	Cost, Insurance and Freight
CPT	Carriage Paid To
CIP	Carriage, Insurance Paid To
DAP	Delivered at Place
DAT	Delivered at Terminal
DDP	Delivered Duty Paid

Incoterms 2020 (IHK Stuttgart, 2025)

overview of the most important Incoterms. "Ex Works" means that the buyer must take care of transport, insurance, and customs clearance from the factory. With "Delivered, Duty Paid", transport, insurance, and customs clearance are the responsibility of the manufacturer and supplier. Transport and customs clearance from China or India to Europe, for example, can account for more than 20% of the actual purchase price; therefore, Incoterms must be an essential part of the negotiations.

9.2.5 *Guarantee and warranty*

Internationally, there may be different warranty periods than those prescribed by German warranty law. Warranty claims and guarantee periods should, therefore, be discussed and agreed upon during negotiations. In particular, replacement times, replacement deliveries, improvements, or repairs must be taken into account here. If you want to comply with legal claims, clauses in international contracts can indicate which country's law applies.

9.2.6 *Due date and default interest*

In business, the due date interest rate, or default interest rate, is an interest rate that a debtor must pay to a creditor by law or contract in the event of late payment. Due date and default interest for possible monetary claims are an essential part of negotiations and should be defined in terms of their amount to be on the safe side in order to take into account the damage and delay in potentially lengthy legal proceedings.

9.2.7 *Currency and payment transactions*

Determining the currency and ensuring incoming payments are key issues in international trade of goods. With the United States alone, Germany generated more than EUR 160 billion in sales in 2021. In addition, other countries such as China, Great Britain, and Switzerland are among the strongest trading partners in the foreign trade balance (AHK, 2018). Even with much smaller Switzerland, foreign trade turnover (imports and exports) amounted to more than EUR 94 billion. Accordingly, around a quarter of all claims and liabilities of German companies against foreign business partners are denominated in a foreign currency, according to the balance of payments statistics of the Deutsche Bundesbank (Deutsche Bank, 2018). Internationally, different rules apply to payment transactions, especially for those outside the eurozone. Thanks to the Single Euro Payments Area (SEPA), money transfers between different European countries are now uncomplicated and inexpensive. However, as soon as orders or invoices are placed in a different currency, entrepreneurs must protect themselves against corresponding exchange rate risks. On the other hand, different payment practices (such as payments from EUR or USD in regulated markets to Asia and Latin America), non-transparent fees, strict reporting requirements, or legal restrictions on foreign exchange transactions can significantly hinder foreign business. This can lead to lost sales, angry customers, or even contractual penalties if a delivery of goods is delayed due to payment problems. Conversely, it can also lead to liquidity disadvantages, unforeseen additional costs, or lost sales opportunities if foreign clients are unable to pay for deliveries and services quickly, securely, and inexpensively.

9.2.8 *Place of jurisdiction and arbitration courts*

In most cases, one of the two countries involved is agreed upon as the place of jurisdiction for international legal transactions. An arbitration clause in contracts is particularly recommended for contracts with a larger scope of delivery and correspondingly higher contract amounts. If an arbitration court is agreed, a national court that is called upon by a contracting party despite the arbitration clause would declare itself incompetent. Arbitration awards are often easier to enforce; arbitration courts are usually faster since they bypass traditional court processes. Arbitration courts are often more appropriate because the arbitrators tend to be experts. Arbitration proceedings are not public (this is important for processes requiring confidentiality). However, although arbitration proceedings can be more expensive than those in state courts, there is still only one court, whereas state courts usually consist of two or even three courts. You may save on translation costs because a German judge can, for example, demand that all English documents be translated into German. Regarding enforceability, there are international agreements to which most of our sales countries have acceded, especially the UN Convention on the Recognition and Enforcement of Foreign Arbitral Awards, to which 137 countries had acceded by 31 December 2005. A list of these countries can be found on the IHK SH website (IHK Schleswig-Holstein, 2025). The following are the best-known "institutional arbitration courts". These are organisations that constantly conduct arbitration proceedings and adopt arbitration rules that regulate the conduct of arbitration proceedings (similar to the Code of Civil Procedure (ZPO), which regulates proceedings before state courts; however, the arbitration rules are not nearly as formally strict as those of the ZPO):

- The best-known international arbitration court is the arbitration court at the International Chamber of Commerce in Paris (International Chamber of Commerce, ICC).
- The International Arbitration Court at the Zurich Chamber of Commerce.
- The Arbitration Court of the Austrian Chamber of Commerce in Vienna, which has gained importance especially in East–West disputes.
- The German Institute for Arbitration e.V. in Cologne (DIS) is also of international importance.
- The Arbitration Institute of the Stockholm Chamber of Commerce.

In international legal transactions, the arbitration court in London (London Court of International Arbitration) or the arbitration court of the United States (American Arbitration Association, AAA) (IHK Schleswig-Holstein, 2025) are important courts. The most important contract elements are summarised in Table 9.2.

Table 9.2. Design of agreement (A-6).

Recording and signing the negotiation results.

Use of both languages of origin or agreement on one language, e.g., English.

Consideration of aspects such as:
- Place of jurisdiction
- Legal aspects/UN Sales Law for international contracts
- Place of performance
- Delivery dates
- Incoterms 2022
- Due date and default interest
- Guarantee cases
- Currency and payment transactions
- Choice of bank

Fast and immediate drafting and ratification of contracts.

Observance and compliance with all negotiated points.

Festive setting at the conclusion of international negotiations.

Successive control and confirmation with the other party that the contract is observed and complied with by both parties.

9.3 Letter of Intent

A letter of intent (LoI) is a non-binding declaration of intent, confirming that the parties to the LoI are in negotiations to conclude a contract. In some cases, an LoI is understood as a unilateral fixation of the sender's negotiating position. In practice, however, the LoI is often used as a document to be signed by both parties (Helmold, 2018). LoIs are used in the run-up to company acquisitions, software contracts, and cooperations, particularly in large projects. They are intended to set out the status of the negotiations and their seriousness; however, they are legally non-binding, i.e., there is no right to conclude the intended contract. An LoI does not establish an obligation to conclude the intended main contract (no binding effect). However, individual provisions of the LoI, such as exclusivity clauses and confidentiality agreements, are binding for the agreed-upon period.

9.4 Memorandum of Understanding

If a declaration of intent is made and signed among several negotiating partners, it is also referred to as a "memorandum of understanding"

(MoU), a term originating in the U.S. legal system. It is also a pure decla-ration of intent, for which the same principles apply as those in an LoI. In practice, the terms are sometimes used synonymously. The title of the document is irrelevant. What is decisive is the content, from which it can be seen that it is a non-binding declaration of intent, i.e., an LoI or an MoU.

9.5 Preliminary Contract

As already shown above, the essential feature of an LoI is that it is a pure declaration of intent with no binding effect. The LoI must therefore be distinguished from a preliminary contract, which obliges the parties to conclude the main contract (Helmold, 2023). The essential contractual components of the later main contract are already regulated in a prelimi-nary contract. In this case, the implementation of the main contract is enforceable, in contrast to the LoI or MoU. It can be sensible to conclude a preliminary contract, for example, if there are still actual or legal obstacles to the main contract (e.g., building permits). In such a case, the obligation to conclude the main contract may be made conditional in the preliminary contract contingent upon a specific event occurring or an obstacle being removed. A preliminary contract can also be designed in such a way that only one party is bound, but the other party has no obliga-tion to conclude the contract.

References

AHK (2018). Außenhandelskammern. Available at: https://www.ahk.de/ [Abgerufen am 3 June 2018].

Deutsche Bank (2025). Internationalen Zahlungsverkehr erfolgreich steuern. Available at: https://www.deutsche-bank.de/ub/unsere-loesungen/zahlungs verkehr/zahlungen-im-in-und-ausland.html.

Helmold, M. (2018). *Erfolgreiche Verhandlungen und Best-in-Class Empfehlungen für den Verhandlungsdurchbruch*. Manuskript und Workshopunterlagen im Master- und MBA-Studium.

Helmold, M. (2023). *Verhandlungen gewinnen. Konzepte, Methoden und Tools*. Cham: Springer.

Helmold, M. *et al.* (2022). *Successful Negotiations. Best-in-Class Recommen-dations for Breakthrough Negotiations*. Wiesbaden: Springer.

IHK Berlin (2018). Internationales Vertragsrecht und UN-Kaufrecht. Available at: https://www.ihk-berlin.de/blob/bihk24/Service-und-Beratung/international/

downloads/2252700/074b1ae0b731ef9780be39c15db30776/UN_Kaufrecht-data.pdf [Abgerufen am 3 June 2018].

IHK Berlin (2025). Incoterms 2020. Available at: https://www.ihk.de/blueprint/servlet/resource/blob/2252702/a05299ee6488328d641699e052be0eee/incoterms-2020-data.pdf [Retrieved 21 March 2025].

IHK Schleswig-Holstein (2025). Ratschläge zur Gestaltung internationaler Verträge. Available at: https://www.ihk.de/schleswig-holstein/international/investitionen/rechtliche-bestimmungen-invest/internationale-vertraege-1372684.

IHK Stuttgart (2025). Die Bedeutung der Incoterms. Available at: https://www.ihk.de/stuttgart/fuer-unternehmen/international/internationales-wirtschaftsrecht/internationale-liefergeschaefte/incoterms/incoterms-2010-684806 [Retrieved 26 February 2025].

Chapter 10

Fairness and Empathy in Negotiations

10.1 Fairness in Negotiations

Fairness refers to decisions and business actions without favouritism or discrimination (Helmold, 2023). Fairness is one of the most important aspects of negotiation. In most negotiations, genuine notions of fairness play a role for reasons that are both intrinsic (ethical) and practical. They help the negotiation parties evaluate options and deals. It is imperative for both parties to assess the fairness of their own proposals from multiple points of view (Albin, 2001).

People of all cultures reject useful deals, believing they are not fair to themselves. We are not only interested in our personal benefits but also constantly advocate for justice. What we perceive as fair and what is not in a negotiation depends not only on the result but also, at least as much, on the process. Fairness expresses an idea of justice. In German, the term "Fairness" can be equated with "accepted justice" and "appropriateness" or with "decency" (Helmold *et al.*, 2024). The Harvard concept aims at fair negotiations, which can be helped by norms of fairness. Fairness norms are also generally of great importance to lawyers. In addition to compiling the various approaches, it is particularly important to determine under which conditions a principle is considered "fair":

- Equality
- Equity
- Need
- *Status quo*

The Duden defines fairness as follows (Duden, 2022): decent behaviour; fair, honest attitude towards others, decent and comradely behaviour in accordance with the rules of the game, in a game, in a competition, etc.

Fairness, therefore, means that a matter should be balanced and should not contradict recognised norms. Essentially, the virtue of fairness sets moral standards for decisions that influence others – so far, so good.

There are no strict legal rules in negotiating. What you can and want to be responsible for is allowed! But how does this fit in with the concept of fairness?

10.2 Value of Fairness in Negotiations

Long-term business partnerships are usually characterised by a great deal of trust that has developed over time. Both sides value what they have in their partners.

Trust refers to the fact that the balance of interests is always and quite naturally established. Fairness is what I see as the lubricant for well-functioning partnerships. This is shown by the fact that, in individual negotiations, there is not always haggling over the last euro, or the partner facing major problems is approached more closely.

He is supported on points that are important to him in the moment, confident of future compensation. In this way, crises can be mastered together.

The danger, however, is that such concessions are systematically exploited. Then, the partnership level becomes unbalanced. I can only recommend keeping a clear eye on this.

10.3 Recommendations for Action when Handling Unfair Negotiating Partners

If you are currently negotiating with long-term business partners and keep facing additional demands, you must react. I can recommend the following three options.

10.3.1 *Set limits for additional requests and demands*

Even in negotiations between partners, there are demands, often requests for concessions, with reference to the partnership. If this becomes one-sided in the long run, then it is important to set limits and also to say "no" and reject requests when the opportunity arises.

10.3.2 *Demand reciprocity*

You can continue to accommodate the other side, but you should make reciprocity binding. You can do this by demanding concessions from the other side. This can be accomplished either as part of the upcoming agreement or as a future agreement.

10.3.3 *Take stock*

If you have already given a lot and now feel disadvantaged, take stock with your counterpart. Write down who has invested what in the interest of the partnership. This action, at the very least, will move those still interested in a real partnership. Otherwise, the partnership would be nothing more than a facade.

10.4 Agree on Fairness Rules

Generally valid norms, recognised standards, or principles can be valid and therefore binding for all negotiation parties involved. Fair criteria can be applied not only to the content of a negotiation but also to the procedure. By using objective criteria, the settlement of conflicts of interest can be avoided according to the "law of the strongest". Fairness rules can be agreed upon before the actual negotiations.

10.5 Ethics in Negotiations

"Ethics" comes from the Greek word "ethos", meaning custom or habit. It deals with activities we typically engage in and examines our perceptions of what we believe to be right and important. Ethics is also part of philosophy and therefore asks why this is so. Ethical action is conscious behaviour that respects societal norms and strives for valuable goals (Helmold *et al.*, 2020). Negotiation ethics involves critical reflections on human actions during negotiations and interactions with negotiating opponents, as long as these are differentiated and assessed according to the ethically good and ethically bad (Francis, 2016). Most companies have codes of ethics in which managers and employees commit themselves to act ethically towards third parties, including during negotiations. In general, codes of ethics or codes of conduct are essentially systematic collections of rules and norms applicable to a professional group or organisation. They primarily specify how the respective employees should behave. The business relationships between companies are referred to as business-to-business, or B2B. The relationships between companies and consumers, however, are called business-to-consumer, or B2C. Another element is corporate social responsibility (CSR), also usually described in a CSR agreement, in which companies commit themselves to advocating social standards, maintaining fairness, and fighting corruption (Dathe *et al.*, 2022). Not least due to consumer movements, companies are becoming increasingly aware of the need to improve their image through CSR activities in relation to B2B partnerships (Fairtrade, 2020). The typical approaches are fair trade and ethical trade.

A company's own CSR profile and value chain are now closely linked to the activities of its stakeholders. In view of the globalisation of business and industry, this is even more true for international business transactions. Business partners must now take responsibility for sustainability in their national and international relationships; they also have a duty to care, as reflected in the negotiations. In concrete terms, this means paying greater attention to ecological, economic, and social aspects (Wunder, 2017). Minimum requirements include compliance with laws, adherence to social standards, consideration of environmental aspects, protection of intellectual property, implementation of occupational health and safety measures, and anti-corruption efforts.

Practical tip: Fairness is not only about the outcome but also about the negotiation process. Make sure the process is fair, talk about how we can negotiate with each other, and demand a fair negotiation process. In negotiations, you should always address the issue of fairness at the beginning. Discussing the questions "When would an agreement be fair for you?" and "What would you base that on?" early in the process can save you a lot of trouble towards the end of the negotiation. It also shows that you possess foresight and a genuine interest in finding a solution that is viable for both sides.

Figure 10.1 shows the elements of CSR, which are important in business transactions and negotiations.

Figure 10.1. CSR and ethics in negotiations.

10.6 Empathy in Negotiations

Empathy is a tool that negotiators can use to increase their negotiation skills. It is also a tool that can cause harm to a negotiator if its usage is mistimed or misperceived.

In negotiations, empathy is the ability to understand and emotionally convey a shared feeling with one's negotiation counterpart. It differs from sympathy in that it is perceived differently; the latter, however, is more of a display of pity.

During negotiations, negotiators can use empathy in a myriad of ways. It can help establish trust, enhance rapport, prevent potential impasses, and create a better negotiating environment (Helmold, 2023).

References

Albin, C. (2001). *Justice and Fairness in International Negotiation.* Cambridge: Cambridge Press.

Dathe, T., *et al.* (2022). *Corporate Social Responsibility (CSR), Sustainability and Environmental Social Governance (ESG). Approaches to Ethical Management.* Cham: Springer.

Duden (2022). Duden. Available at: https://www.duden.de/ [Abgerufen am 12 July 2022].

Fairtrade.de (2020). Was ist fairer Handel? Available at: https://www.fairtrade.de/ index.php/mID/1.1/lan/de#Mehr_als_nur_ein_fairer_Preis [Abgerufen am 2 January 2020].

Francis, R. (2016). Ethical Risk Management. In F. A. (eds), *Global Encyclopedia of Public Administration, Public Policy, and Governance*. Cham: Springer.

Helmold, M. (2023). *Verhandlungen gewinnen. Konzepte, Methoden und Tools*. Cham: Springer.

Helmold, M., *et al.* (2020). *Corporate Social Responsibility im internationalen Kontext.*

Helmold, M., *et al.* (2024). *ESG, CSR und SDG als langfristiger Wettbewerbsvorteil. Nachhaltigkeit durch innovative Konzepte, Methoden und Tools*. Wiesbaden: Springer.

Wunder, R. (2017). *CSR und Strategisches Management. Wie man mit Nachhaltigkeit langfristig im Wettbewerb gewinnt*. Wiesbaden: Springer.

Chapter 11

Stress in Negotiations

11.1 The Win-Win Situation

Stress in negotiations arises when negotiation goals cannot fully or partly be achieved (Helmold, 2023). The process of negotiating demands good business judgement and a keen understanding of human nature. There is no other area in business where the alchemy of power, persuasion, economics, motivation, and organisational pressures come together in such a concentrated fashion and within such a narrow time frame.

Negotiators often focus on potential threats and negative outcomes of a negotiation, ruminating on how they might fail. This "threat mindset" leads them to feel anxious, making failure more likely.

In situations where the benefits are obvious to both parties, there are usually no differences. This is called a "win-win" situation, as shown in the illustration in Figure 11.1. If a successful manufacturer secures a new sales opportunity, both parties achieve high added value. This also applies to a new project, where both partners can give each other help to reduce risk. Any good addition to one's own position by another represents a win-win situation. If the partners disclose their interests, the objects of interest are often expanded during the negotiation. The partner's processes and services can be evaluated and related to one's own potential. This approach also corresponds to the strategy of "enlarging the pie", which can support the success of a negotiation. Far too often, negotiating positions are shaped by short-term negotiation goals or personal attitudes. This leads to win-lose negotiations that are rarely repeated. Negotiations are a tool for securing the future. Before starting negotiations, both sides

Figure 11.1.   Win-win, win-lose, lose-lose, and lose-win.

should ask themselves how important the relationship with their partner is to them and what contribution the other side makes to their own well-being. If both sides are able to articulate their interests, viable solutions emerge rather than short-lived compromises that leave neither side satisfied. Negotiations conducted according to the win-win principle usually lead to a lasting relationship that is characterised by long-term added value for both sides. The win-win principle is also worthwhile in negotiations whose success is not clearly foreseeable. Because it maintains an equal position for further negotiations, even if one side should achieve significantly greater success.

Figure 11.1 shows the respective concepts of win-win, win-lose, lose-win, and lose-lose in negotiations. If both parties' interests are well balanced and both sides achieve a high degree of goal achievement (our side and the opposing interests), a win-win situation has been achieved. However, if one party is not completely satisfied because the goals have not been achieved to their full satisfaction, this is referred to as a win-lose or lose-win situation. The boundaries of the concepts are often fluid, and the degree to which goals are achieved can be based on dynamic, macroeconomic, or microeconomic changes.

11.2 Win-Win as an Illusion in Negotiations

The win-win concept has been described for decades in numerous negotiation books and seminars and offered by trainers as a means of resolving conflicts. This concept comes from game theory and is also known in the field of negotiation as the "Harvard concept" and in conflict mediation as "conflict resolution without losers" (Helmold, 2023). This principle states that it would be possible to find results that would allow both parties to emerge as winners despite their initially opposing interests (Bauer-Jelinek, 2007). Furthermore, the win-win strategy is based on the willingness of the negotiators to achieve common and lasting solutions by not insisting on superficial positions but rather revealing their underlying motives (Schranner, 2009). To achieve this, all parties must have high-level communication skills, and the atmosphere must be reasonably trusting and harmonious (Bosch, 2022). Even the proponents of the theory assert that a win-win approach is more likely to succeed when the differences in the parties' interests are not too great (Helmold *et al.*, 2022). However, practical experience from negotiation experts shows that in the case of conflicts of interest in business or politics, both parties try to get the maximum out of it for themselves; there is rarely a chance of a real win for both sides (Bauer-Jelinek, 2007). Especially in cases where there are budget restrictions or when a project involves multiple interested parties and suppliers, negotiation positions are often adopted that are not viewed as win-win but rather as win-lose. In contrast to the win-win principle, the win-lose concept involves one negotiating party that is not a winner.

As long as there are enough people who are not only concerned with their own advantage but also value a fair balance of interests in negotiations, their attitude can be used to a great extent to assert one's own interests. Those who want to achieve the maximum (negotiation maximisers) in their objectives use a deceptive manoeuvre by appealing to the notion of common gain. The maximum (from Latin, meaning "the most") includes the greatest possible negotiation success and the maximum achievement of negotiation goals for the negotiator or negotiation maximiser (Bauer-Jelinek, 2007). While the fair negotiating partner is still looking for common ground, the negotiation maximiser has already presented his positions. And if he has mastered the win-win technique well, the "do-gooder" only realises much later that his gains are worth little or nothing.

The following case study should explain this in more detail (Bauer-Jelinek, 2007). An employee in procurement or sales who has worked for a company for two years and achieved significant success in meeting his budget goals. The savings have fundamentally improved the department's business results. The employee has several years of professional experience but has been with the company for only two years. During his performance review, the employee expects a bonus or a raise as a result of his savings. He expects that his manager will approach him; however, the manager does not approach the employee. The employee then decides to approach his manager, who, however, has his own goals in mind and wants to appease the employee with a "win-win deal". With the budget savings, a new employee in sales is hired to handle the high workload. The manager puts the employee off until better times and the next fiscal year. He also says that additional resources would ensure job security in difficult economic periods. In his discussion, he emphasises common interests, especially the well-being of the company in the long term, and ends the discussion in a friendly manner. The employee is now in a dilemma. Should he abandon his motive and accept the offer so that new resources can be hired, or should he continue to push for a raise? Practical examples, such as the one just mentioned, show that the win-win situation is usually merely an illusion. In this case, the manager has won the negotiations. Savings and reaching the budget help him to further expand his department; however, the employee receives no benefit at all. His job has not really become more secure, and due to his very good performance, the individual targets for the following financial year may even be increased further.

11.3 Targeted Use of Stress and Conflict Situations

Negotiators must process a large amount of data and background information simultaneously while making complex decisions within a short span, which systematically influences the further course of the negotiation. In parallel, they must consider all necessary information to achieve their set minimum goals. Often, time constraints or a lack of resources lead to pressure on the negotiators. This automatically triggers stress and stressful situations.

While mild eustress (positive stress) ensures that we are more efficient in decision-making situations, we must be wary of distress (negative stress) in negotiations. Because if the levels of stress hormones adrenaline, noradrenaline, and cortisol increase with psychological pressure, their positive effect is reversed. Stuttering, a lack of concentration, and blackouts are the consequences. The more the brain is stressed, the more it promotes more irrational behaviour.

Modern concepts recommend the conscious, targeted triggering of stressful situations. To achieve this, you can deliberately trigger conflicts in order to trigger stress on the other side. Stress is supposed to prepare the mind and body for fight or flight. When stress symptoms occur, negotiation partners often lose track of the situation and reveal weaknesses through careless actions or non-verbal signals (Helmold, 2023).

11.4 Effects on Stress

Stress can have a wide range of effects on the body, mind, and behaviour. Physically, negative stress can manifest itself in various forms, including cardiovascular disorders, migraines, diabetes, heartburn, and stomach ulcers. Psychologically, negative stress can cause feelings of helplessness and exhaustion (Sies, 2019). This can lead to mental illnesses, such as depression or anxiety disorders. Negative consequences of dealing with one's social environment and job are also possible.

11.5 Eustress and Distress

Eustress and distress refer to different types of stress. Eustress feels challenging, yet manageable, and leads to growth, while distress is difficult and has a negative impact (Figure 11.2).

Eustress is recognised as a positive driver for achieving negotiation goals. Eustress is usually associated with situations in which we feel a sense of control and believe that the stressor is something we can handle (Cooper, 2013). Distress is often linked to situations in which we feel a lack of control and perceive the stressor as a threat.

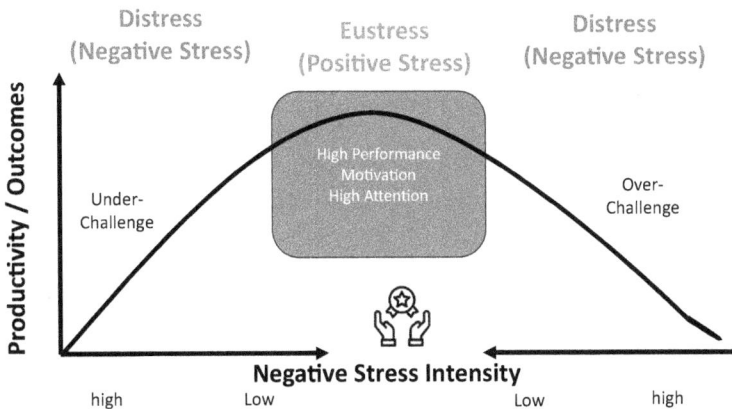

Figure 11.2. Eustress and distress.

- Eustress increases attention: you become more concentrated and focused on your topic.
- Eustress promotes performance and productivity during negotiations: your muscles become more tense, and your entire body is ready to react. This helps with a challenging task on the computer, as well as intense strength training.
- Eustress motivates: have you mastered a challenge? The happiness hormone, dopamine, is released. Congratulations! That increases your motivation.
- Eustress increases self-confidence: if you solve several problems, this leads to a good feeling of successfully completing tasks.

Practical tip: To incorporate eustress into your negotiations, consider pushing yourself outside your comfort zone, learning something new, or taking on an additional responsibility. Adopt a positive attitude towards stress by facing new challenges with a confident mindset, breathing through difficult moments, and using positive self-talk.

References

Bauer-Jelinek, C. (2007). *Die geheimen Spielregeln der Macht und die Illusionen der Gutmenschen.* Salzburg: Ecowin Verlag.

Bosch, T. (2022). Die Harvard-Illusion von der Win-Win-Verhandlungsstrategie. Available at: https://bosch-ag.com/die-harvard-illusion-von-der-win-win-verhandlungsstrategie/.

Cooper, C. L. (2013). *From Stress to Wellbeing. The Theory and Research on Occupational Stress and Wellbeing*, Volume 1. London: Palgrave McMillan.

Helmold, M. (2023). *Verhandlungen gewinnen. Konzepte, Methoden und Tools.* Cham: Springer.

Helmold, M., Dathe, T., and Hummel, F. (2022). *Successful Negotiations: Best-in-Class Recommendations for Breakthrough Negotiations.* Wiesbaden: Springer.

Schranner, M. (2009). Ratgeber. Die sieben größten Fehler in Verhandlungen. Available at: https://www.wiwo.de/erfolg/trends/ratgeber-die-sieben-groessten-fehler-in-verhandlungen/5574408.html [Abgerufen am 7 June 2022].

Sies, H. (2019). *Oxidative Stress. Eustress and Distress.* Cambridge, Massachusetts: Academic Press.

Chapter 12

The FBI Concept as Successful Trigger in Negotiations (ETIB)

12.1 Empathy, Trust, Influence, and Change

12.1.1 *The principle*

Taking the power of persuasion, empathy, and active listening can help achieve breakthroughs in negotiations (Voss and Raz, 2017). A successful concept is the ETIB methodology. ETIB, as shown in Figure 12.1, stands for empathy, trust, influence, and (behavioural) change. The ETIB strategy is based on the FBI's staircase model and thus represents a recommended

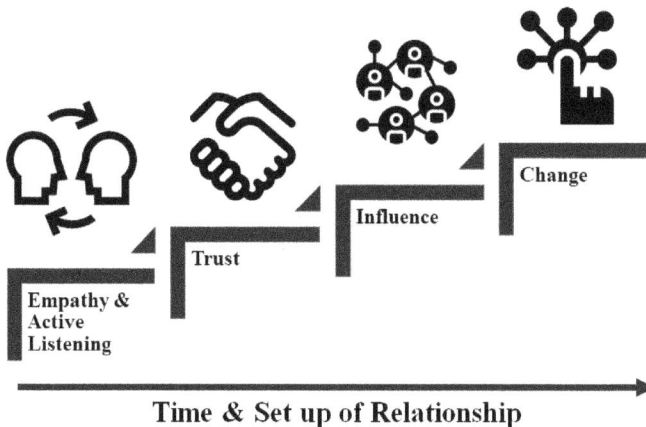

Figure 12.1.   The FBI negotiation concept.

and structured sequence for every professionally conducted negotiation. Accordingly, every negotiation begins with bonding, in which trust is built through tactical empathy (Hofmann, 2018). Once this level has been reached, negotiators can mention their mission and move on to the next step of influencing. In order to build at least a 51% trust level, clearly defined tactics must be consistently implemented step-by-step in the same way.

12.1.2 *Level 1: Empathy*

Level 1 is the starting point and involves "empathy" and "active listening". In doing so, you try to understand your negotiating partner.

Make statements that show your negotiating partner that you are listening to them intensively. Active listening statements include the following:

- minimal agreement (e.g., "ah", "ooh", "uuh") (or "minimal encouragements"),
- repeating words or parts of sentences ("mirroring"),
- summarising content ("paraphrasing"),
- repeating emotions ("emotional labelling"), and
- repeating content and emotions ("summarising").

12.1.3 *Level 2: Trust*

The second level is "tactical empathy"; in doing so, you communicate to your negotiating partner that you understand them. This is how trust is built. This process is called "bonding". Bonding is a process in which you work on building trust with your negotiating partner and gathering as much information about them as possible. A key finding of the FBI is that, without trust, one cannot influence others or change their (previous) decisions. Bonding can occur in as little as seconds; however, it may last from minutes to hours or even extend over days. Bonding can also "break down" in a matter of seconds; then, you start again (ask questions, listen, summarise, and communicate understanding).

12.1.4 *Level 3: Influence*

These two tactics (active listening and tactical empathy) ideally lead to level 3 (at least 51% trust), i.e., a state in which trust in you exceeds mistrust. Now it is time to initiate influence.

12.1.5 *Level 4: Behavioural change*

Level 4 targets behavioural change. From now on, you have the opportunity to influence your partner in relation to your mission. An effective way to influence is anchoring: state a specific amount as your desired salary. This sets a reference point. Your negotiating partner then begins to adjust from this reference point, namely, in the categories of "too high" or "too low".

12.2 The FBI Principle: Never Negotiate Alone

12.2.1 *Together we are strong*

In a difficult negotiation situation, it is easy to lose sight of things, perhaps even react heatedly and emotionally – resulting in correspondingly negative consequences for the negotiation outcome. It is therefore advisable to sit at the negotiating table as a team (Helmold *et al.*, 2019). However, this can also have risks. If the negotiating team does not act in coordination, the plan can easily backfire. The team should, therefore, decide together in advance whom or which roles they will assume and prepare the negotiation strategy (Neumann, 2019). Numerous negotiation experts use the FBI's approach in their negotiation concepts. Agents conduct difficult negotiations in teams for the simple reason that those who negotiate alone might be too fixated on their negotiation goals. They concentrate solely on their strategy and arguments, overlooking analytical listening and observation. In a very tense negotiation situation, they can therefore miss important observations. In FBI negotiations, a second person takes on these tasks.

12.2.2 *Negotiation in a team of three*

In a project, too, distributed roles, with each having clear tasks assigned to them, can make negotiations easier. The following roles have proven to be effective:

- The negotiator assumes the role of one who sets the agenda and makes demands.
- The commander primarily listens, thinks strategically, and ensures the team adheres to the previously agreed-upon negotiation line.
- The decision-maker has the final say on how to proceed and is responsible for the result.

The negotiator, to the outside world, appears as the sole contact person for the other side (Helmold *et al.*, 2022). However, he does not make decisions alone. His goal is to build emotional closeness and trust with his counterpart. Since emotional relationships are not a one-way street, he is vulnerable to compromise; this is because, as he develops understanding, making entirely rational decisions becomes increasingly challenging. It has therefore proven to be effective for another person to decide on the results (Helmold, 2023). At the beginning of the negotiation, the negotiator therefore points out that important decisions require consultation.

Practical tip: Use the FBI concept with tactical empathy to influence and change the behaviour of your negotiation opponent. Try to understand the negotiation partner through empathy and active listening. Based on trust, influence and behavioural change are possible.

References

Helmold, M. (2023). *Verhandlungen gewinnen. Konzepte, Methoden und Tools.* Cham: Springer.

Helmold, M., Dathe, T., and Hummel, F. (2019). *Erfolgreiche Verhandlungen. Best-in-Class Empfehlungen für den Verhandlungsdurchbruch.* Wiesbaden: Springer.

Helmold, M., Dathe, T., and Hummel, F. (2022). *Successful Negotiations. Best-in-Class Recommendations for Breakthrough Negotiations.* Cham: Springer.

Hofmann, T. (2018). *Das FBI-Prinzip: Verhandlungstaktiken für Gewinner.* München: Ariston.

Neumann, M. (2019). Schlagkräftiger im Team. Verhandeln nach der FBI-Methode. Available at: https://www.projektmagazin.de/artikel/fbi-methode-verhandlung [Abgerufen am 28 June 2022].

Voss, C. and Raz, T. (2017). *Never Split the Difference: Negotiating As If Your Life Depended On It.* Harper Business.

Chapter 13

Active and Analytical Listening

13.1 What is Active and Analytical Listening?

13.1.1 Subject and definition

Successful negotiators carefully check whether the negotiation opponent is satisfied with their positions as well (Helmold, 2023). Considering the self-esteem of the negotiation opponent is a key factor in successful negotiations (Opresnik, 2014). The active and analytical listening method is a suitable concept for understanding the other negotiation motives and interests. Active and analytical listening during negotiations is understood as the emotional (affective) reaction of a conversation partner to a message from the negotiating partner. Active listening involves an emotional and factual response from the listener, taking into account both the emotions conveyed by the speaker and the content of their message. In essence, it is about not merely listening passively and allowing the other person to speak but also staying active, even when you are not speaking yourself. The information received is also analysed through questions – for comprehension and the reaction of the negotiating partner (Nichols, 2018). Information can be verified and confirmed by asking similar counterquestions. There are also suitable strategies, tactics, and questioning techniques. Active and analytical listening means an open, active, respectful, and empathetic attitude towards the conversation partner and its content. This means that you should listen carefully to your conversation partner, agree with them, and, if necessary, ask questions about what they are saying but without interrupting the other person. Active listening is one of the most effective communication techniques for successful

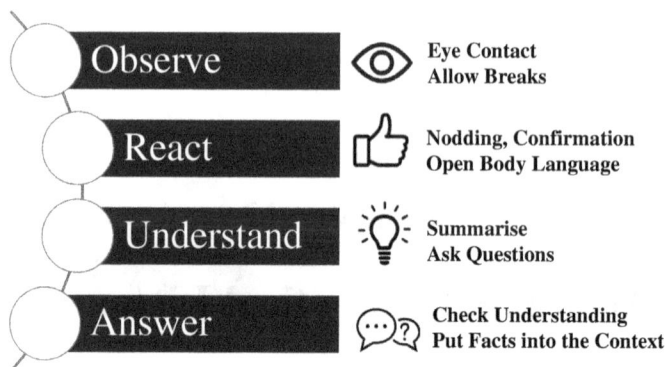

Figure 13.1. Active and analytical listening.

negotiations (Guszkowski, 2018). Active listening is an essential component of modern and innovative negotiation concepts. This method aims to obtain as much information as possible from the negotiating opponent and to reveal as little information about yourself. On the other hand, the concept also serves a deeply human need, namely, to be understood. Anyone who can convey this feeling to their negotiating partner has as good as won. The concept of active and analytical listening, as depicted in Figure 13.1, is structured in four steps.

13.1.2 *Observation and perception*

In the first step, the behaviour and statements of the negotiating opponent are observed and perceived. It is important not only to concentrate on the factual statements of the conversation partner but also to observe and interpret their posture, facial expressions, and gestures (Helmold *et al.*, 2022). Eye contact and pauses help the conversation partner by allowing them time to organise their thoughts and articulate themselves in detail in a relaxed atmosphere.

13.1.3 *React*

The second step is the reaction. Agreement, conveyed through a slight nod, is a way of giving the negotiating opponent the feeling that you are listening attentively. In this step, the method of mirroring is usually helpful. In the conversation, you can mirror both body language and content. Light, brief paraphrasing can also be a suitable technique.

13.1.4 *Understanding and interpreting*

In the third step, the statements of your conversation partner are interpreted and then compared to your own values and experiences. Here, the factual and emotional aspects of the speech of the negotiating opponent are accepted and interpreted based on one's own and social values.

13.1.5 *Answers*

The last step is to react with a careful and well-chosen answer. The reaction to the speech is to reproduce what was said in an appropriate form. In doing so, one focuses on the points that, from one's own perspective, are important and useful for advancing the conversation. When "paraphrasing", one repeats information or arguments from the communication partner in one's own words. It is best to formulate the question from here in order to enable possible corrections. ("Did I understand you correctly that.....? Did you mean....? Did you mean this....?")

Here, one addresses the emotional, hidden messages in the conversation. One expresses the presumed moods and emotions of the conversation partner in one's own words. This only applies if the conversation situation allows it. You should make sure that the nuances are set correctly. It is not what is said but rather how it is said that is interesting above all. This refers to the tone of voice, the manner of speaking, and the speed of speech. It is important that this be your perception and that you should be prepared to accept corrections and objections.

Practical tip: Combine active listening with a touch of humour. Humour makes your life easier; it humanises your communication and creates closeness. People who act and react with humour are seen as more likeable and trustworthy. Communication can be fun! Humour is also a good way to let off steam, especially when things aren't going so well.

13.2 Advantages of Active and Analytical Listening

When actively listening, the listener reflects both factual and emotional aspects of one's speech back to the other person. Especially when dealing with difficult and emotional topics, this form of conversation builds mutual trust and thus improves communication (Hoffmann, 2018). Active listening also makes it possible to initiate a change in the other person's behaviour.

13.2.1 *Communication*

If you allow your opponent to speak more, you will not only receive gratitude but also many tips on how to conduct the negotiation in the final phase. By that time, you will have accomplished three significant milestones through active listening: your own competence will be recognised, you will be valued as an individual, and the trust in your opponent will increase. This results in several advantages for further communication.

13.2.2 *Influencing orientation*

Analytical listening helps in grasping the opponent's main points. Now, it is simply a matter of aligning it with your personal objectives and assigning value based on your own interests.

13.2.3 *Moderating the content*

The interim summaries place the negotiating partner, who has been actively listening, into a second role: that of the moderator. This, naturally, also includes a neutral position that the negotiating partner now subliminally acknowledges. The moderator, however, takes over the leadership of the conversation.

13.2.4 *Controlling the results*

If 90% of the negotiation has already been conducted using an integrative strategy, it is unlikely to change in the last few minutes. The negotiating partner has been drawn into the active listener's pull and, therefore, will likely make only minor attempts to alter the emerging negotiation result. If the active listener has done thorough preparatory work, he may even show conciliation here. The negotiating partner leaves the negotiation feeling satisfied, despite not having achieved his goals. But the most important thing is that he will always seek negotiations with the active listener. This interaction is fundamental to successful negotiations and should be a part of every negotiation training!

13.3 Techniques and Recommendations for Active Listening

13.3.1 *Show acceptance and agreement*

As everyone knows, communication only works as long as one party speaks and the other listens. But is it enough merely to listen, especially with more complex topics? Everyone has caught themselves drifting off while the other person talks to them. How do you prevent this, and how do you get the maximum amount of information from a conversation?

Nobody likes talking to a wall. So, actively convey to your conversation partner that you are interested in listening to them. Techniques and methods include maintaining eye contact, nodding, repeating what has been said, and asking questions.

13.3.2 *Remain open and empathetic towards your conversation partner*

Create an open, relaxed atmosphere. Show that you are open to other opinions and do not judge in a biased way. Your counterpart should feel that you have compassion for them and understand different ways of thinking. Leave your own opinions aside for the moment; listening is solely concerned with gathering information from the negotiation partner. Techniques and methods are an open-body posture, not criticism or interpretation.

13.3.3 *Avoid distractions*

Associative listening is the exact opposite of active listening. You may be listening, but your mind wanders, and the information literally goes "in one ear and out the other". Techniques and methods provide a quiet place for discussion; don't get distracted by irritating words, don't get carried away emotionally, and don't interpret and filter out the information soberly.

13.3.4 *Don't allow yourself to be under time pressure*

As soon as you are under time pressure, you stop listening. While you are listening, you only think about your answer in order to end the conversation as quickly as possible. In doing so, you lose half of the information. Take the time for a longer conversation, especially in today's times when digital communication is increasingly taking precedence.

13.4 Question Forms and Techniques for Active and Analytical Listening

In addition to strong rhetorical skills, negotiation experts must also listen actively and analytically to their negotiating partner with empathy (Hofmann, 2018). Empathy is the ability and willingness to recognise and understand the feelings, thoughts, opinions, motives, personality traits, character traits, or intercultural characteristics of the negotiating opponent and to direct their activities accordingly. The questioning techniques shown in Table 13.1 support negotiations.

Table 13.1.   Question types in negotiations.

Question Types	Example	Question Behaviour	Effects
Leading questions	You are of the opinion that...?	Externally determining	Confirming, controlling
Open questions	What do you say to that...?	Partnership-based	Liberating, supportive
Reflective questions	If I understand correctly, then you mean that...?	Trusting improving	Atmospherically reflective
Directional questions	So you said that...?	Initiating self-determination	Controlling from within
Closed questions	Are you of the opinion that...?	Dominating	Goal-oriented, restrictive
Trick questions	Wasn't your opinion just now that...?	Suspicious	Critical, disruptive

13.5 The Four Dimensions of Active Listening

13.5.1 *Information*

Active listening means showing the speaker that you understand the content of what he is saying and that you are following it carefully. This can be demonstrated through short affirmative interjections or questions; however, it may also involve a slightly bent-forward posture and constant eye contact. Short notes help to summarise what has been said briefly when you start speaking yourself. This gives the other person the assurance that their information has "got through".

13.5.2 *The appeal*

It is even more important for the speaker that his wishes have been understood. He appeals to the negotiating partner to follow these. Since he has combined the appeal with information, confirmation that the negotiating partner has taken in the information equates to an understanding of their wishes concerning the speaker.

13.5.3 *Self-revelation*

Those who speak more reveal more about themselves. The more they reveal themselves, the more transparent they become. Active listening is a clever method that enables one to grasp and analyse the information between the lines. For the speaker, however, the impression is created that the listener is becoming his confidant. This further increases the prospect of favourable negotiation results.

13.5.4 *The relationship level*

From the speaker's language, the negotiating partner can see what value the opponent places on the relationship. Active listening can increase appreciation. At the end of the negotiation, this aspect plays a key role because the negotiation result is also influenced by how you want to deal with each other in the future.

Anyone who knows these four sides of the so-called "communication square" can use them for their own purposes. In contrast, it becomes clear why so many misunderstandings arise in communication: the partners perceive only one level.

Practical tips for active listening

- Adopt an open, facing posture towards your negotiating partner.
- Ensure sufficient eye contact and look at your negotiating partner.
- Nodding signals that you are actively following the conversation.
- Taking notes is a sign of active listening. However, make sure to keep making eye contact.
- Mirror your conversation partner in gestures, posture, clothing, and language. But don't overdo it. Stay authentic.

References

Guszkowski, K. (2018). *Effect of Negotiator Active Listening Skills on Crisis (hostage) Negotiations*. Nova Southeastern University.

Helmold, M. (2023). *Verhandlungen gewinnen. Konzepte, Methoden und Tools.* Cham: Springer.

Helmold, M., Dathe, T., and Hummel, F. (2022). *Successful Negotiations. Best-in-Class Recommendations for Breakthrough Negotiations*. Cham: Springer.

Hofmann, T. (2018). *Das FBI-Prinzip: Verhandlungstaktiken für Gewinner.* München: Ariston.

Nichols, M. (2018). *Die Macht des Zuhörens: Wie man richtiges Zuhören lernt und Beziehungen stärkt.* Kandern: Narayana.

Opresnik, M. O. (2014). *The Hidden Rules of Successful Negotiation and Communication. Getting to Yes!* Heidelberg: Springer.

Chapter 14

Game Theory and the Prisoner's Dilemma in Negotiations

14.1 What is Game Theory

Game theory is the science of strategy and anticipation. It attempts to determine mathematically and logically what actions negotiators should take by predicting the moves of their negotiation opponents (Helmold, 2023). Game theory is intended to formally describe how rational players engage in strategic interactions. As a sub-discipline of game theory, mathematical negotiation theory deals with the situation of a negotiation between two or more parties. Game theory is one of the decision theories. With the help of mathematical models, decision situations are modelled, and the optimal strategies for decision-makers are determined, assuming that all participants behave rationally. An important aspect of game theory is that the outcome depends on the decisions of all participants. This means that the result for one participant also depends on the decisions of the other participants (Holler *et al.*, 2019).

14.2 Prisoner's Dilemma: Subject and Definition

John Nash expanded game theory through his work on non-cooperative games. The Nash equilibrium, named after him, is a solution concept for games with two or more participants in which an optimal solution is achieved when all players know the optimal strategies of the other players and no player can gain an advantage by unilaterally changing their strategy. In certain games, this solution concept leads to a Pareto-inferior solution – the best known being the prisoner's dilemma – where the individually optimal strategy leads to the worst possible solution for all parties involved. The prisoner's dilemma is an example of negotiation in game theory. It models the situation of two prisoners who are accused of committing a crime together. The two prisoners are questioned individually and cannot communicate with one another. If both deny the crime, both receive a low sentence since they can only be proven to have committed an offence that is less severely punished (Axelrod, 1980). If both confess, they will each receive a heavy sentence; however, neither will face the maximum sentence because of their confession. However, if only one of the two prisoners confesses, that person will be exempt from punishment as a key witness, while the other, a convicted but non-confessed offender, will receive the maximum sentence (Tucker, 1983).

The dilemma now consists of the fact that each prisoner must decide whether to either deny (i.e., try to cooperate with the other prisoner) or confess (i.e., betray the other) without knowing the other prisoner's decision. However, the sentence ultimately imposed depends on how the two prisoners testified together and thus depends not only on their own decision but also on the decision of the other prisoner (Wenski, 2019).

The most important premises of the prisoner's dilemma are that the two players behave absolutely rationally and each is regarded as a "homo economicus", which applies to all game theory models. They cannot communicate with each other, so no negotiations can take place. Therefore, each participant must assume that the other is behaving either selfishly or rationally (and confessing).

The prisoner's dilemma is a symmetrical game with complete information, which can be represented in normal form. The dominant strategy for both prisoners is to confess. This combination also represents the only Nash equilibrium. On the other hand, cooperation between the prisoners would lead to a lower sentence for both and thus also to a lower total sentence (Poundstone, 1992).

Two prisoners are suspected of having committed a crime together. Both prisoners are interrogated in separate rooms and have no opportunity to consult each other or coordinate their behaviour. The maximum sentence for the crime is six years. If the prisoners decide to remain silent (cooperation), both are sentenced to two years in prison for minor offences. However, if both confess to the crime (defection), both face a prison sentence; however, due to their cooperation with the investigating

Temptation	Betrayal if the other remains silent (defection in cooperation)	1 Year in Prison	−1
Reward	Keep quiet when the other person is silent (cooperation when cooperating)	2 Years in Prison	−2
Punishment	Betrayal if the other person also betrays (defection in case of defection)	4 Years in Prison	−4
Reward of the Gullible	Keep quiet when the other person betrays (cooperation in the event of defection)	6 Years in Prison	−6

Figure 14.1. Prisoner's dilemma: options.

authorities, they will not receive the maximum sentence but only four years in prison (see Figure 14.1).

If only one of them confesses (defection) and the other remains silent (cooperation), the one who confesses becomes a key witness and receives a one-year suspended sentence, whereas the other receives the maximum sentence of six years in prison. A player's payout therefore depends not only on his own decision but also on that of his accomplice (interdependence of behaviour). Collectively, it is objectively more advantageous for both to remain silent. If both prisoners cooperate, each would only have to go to prison for two years. The loss for both of them combined amounts to four years, and any other combination of confession and silence leads to a greater loss. Individually, it seems more advantageous for both to testify. For each prisoner, the situation is as follows: if the other confesses, his statement reduces the sentence from six to four years; however, if the other remains silent, his statement can reduce the sentence from two to one year! From an individual's perspective, the recommended strategy is definitely to confess. This statement does not depend on the other's behaviour, and it seems to always be more advantageous to confess. Such a strategy, which is chosen regardless of the opponent's, is called a "dominant strategy" in game theory.

The dilemma is based on the fact that collective and individual analyses result in different recommendations for action.

The game structure prevents communication and provokes a one-sided betrayal, through which the traitor hopes to achieve the better result for himself: "one year" (if the fellow prisoner remains silent) or four instead of six years (if the fellow prisoner confesses). If both prisoners pursue this strategy, however, they make their situation worse as a whole– also individually – because they now each receive four years in prison instead of two. This divergence of possible strategies creates the

Prisoner's Dilemma

	B Do Not Confess		B Confess	
A **Do Not** **Confess**	A: -2	B: -2	A: -1	B: -6
	-4 years		-7 years	
A **Confess**	A: -1	B: -6	A: -4	B: -4
	-7 years		-8 years	

Figure 14.2. Prisoner's dilemma: outcomes.

prisoner's dilemma. The supposedly rational, step-by-step analysis of the situation leads both prisoners to confess, which leads to a bad result (suboptimal allocation). The better result could be achieved through cooperation, but this is vulnerable to a breach of trust. The rational players meet at the point where the dominant strategies intersect. This point is known as the Nash equilibrium. The paradox is that both players have no reason to deviate from the Nash equilibrium, although the Nash equilibrium is not a Pareto-optimal state here. Figure 14.2 shows the outcomes and total years of prison for Prisoners A and B.

14.3 The Role of Trust

The prisoner's dilemma stems from their lack of knowledge about the other prisoner's behaviour. Game theory deals with optimal strategies in the prisoner's dilemma. The optimal strategy for both would be to trust each other and cooperate. Trust can be established in two ways: first, through communication – not permitted under the rules of the game – and corresponding proofs of trust, and second, by punishing the other player in the event of a breach of trust (Helmold *et al.*, 2022). In his work, *The Strategy of Conflict*, the economist and game theorist Thomas Schelling addresses such problems under the conditions of the Cold War ("equilibrium of terror"). The punishment for a breach of trust would have been so severe that it would not have been worth it. When playing the prisoner's dilemma repeatedly, most strategies rely on using information from previous rounds. If the other person cooperates in a round, the successful tit-for-tat strategy trusts that he will continue to do so and gives a sign of trust in return. In the opposite case, it punishes to prevent it from being exploited (Helmold *et al.*, 2019).

14.4 The Role of Guilt and Innocence

In the prisoner's dilemma, the question of actual guilt or innocence is excluded. For example, a prisoner always benefits from making a confession, even if he confesses when he is actually innocent. On the other hand, he achieves a worse outcome if moral concerns and the hope of proving his innocence prevent him from confessing (Helmold *et al.*, 2019). If the penalty for not confessing is very high, even innocent people tend to confess; this effect is particularly evident in show trials.

References

Axelrod, A. (1980). Effective choice in the prisoner's dilemma. *Journal of Conflict Resolution*, 24(1), 3–25.

Helmold, M. (2023). *Verhandlungen gewinnen. Konzepte, Methoden und Tools.* Cham: Springer.

Helmold, M., Dathe, T., and Hummel, F. (2019). *Erfolgreiche Verhandlungen: Best-in-Class Empfehlungen für den Verhandlungsdurchbruch.* Wiesbaden: Springer.

Helmold, M., Dathe, T., and Hummel, F. (2022). *Successful Negotiations: Best-in-Class Recommendations for Breakthrough Negotiations.* Cham: Springer.

Holler, M. J., Illing, G., and Napel, S. (2019). *Einführung in die Spieltheorie.* Wiesbaden: Springer.

Poundstone, W. (1992). *Prisoner's Dilemma: John von Neumann, Game Theory, and the Puzzle of the Bomb.* Anchor/Random House.

Tucker, A. W. (1983). A two-person dilemma – The prisoner's dilemma. In P. D. Straffin, *The Mathematics of Tucker – A Sampler. Two-Year College Mathematics Journal*, 14(3), 228–232.

Wenski, G. (2019). Spieltheorie. In *Beraterverkauf im globalen B2B-Equipmentgeschäft. Anleitung für professionelle Verhandlungen im In- und Ausland.* Wiesbaden: Springer.

Chapter 15

Non-Verbal Signals in Negotiations

15.1 Subject of Non-Verbal Communication

Non-verbal communication refers to the part of interpersonal communication that is not conveyed through literal language. It works through certain channels, such as facial expressions, gestures, posture, and voice. It can be intentional or unintentional and perceived consciously or unconsciously. For trained negotiators, decoding methods help identify behavioural patterns and signals, enabling them to draw conclusions from them (Raschl, 2021). Non-verbal communication can be intentional or unintentional; it can provide information about possible deception, stress, or other signals. Motor skills, gestures, facial expressions, choice of words, tone of voice, and body language are ultimately even more important for deciphering true motives and interests than what is said. The so-called micro expressions play a special role in this context since, unlike normal body language, they cannot be consciously controlled. Micro expressions are very easy to recognise for the trained eye. They are fleeting facial expressions that are visible only for a fraction of a second (40–500 ms). And they all have a neurological trigger.

15.2 Types of Non-Verbal Communication

15.2.1 *Kinesics (physical signals of non-verbal communication)*

Kinesics is the science of physical, non-verbal communication behaviour with regard to human motor skills, gestures, facial expressions,

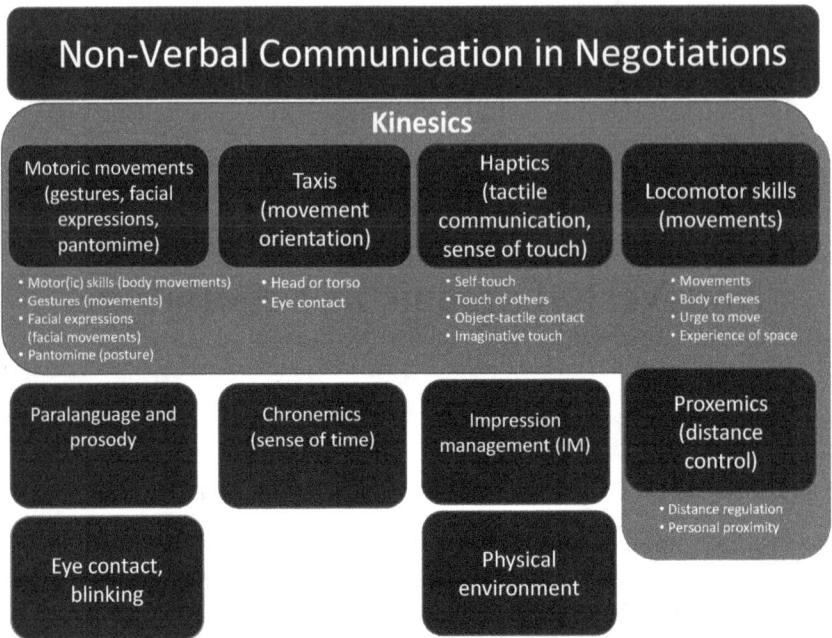

Figure 15.1.   Types of non-verbal communication.

pantomime, taxis, haptics, locomotor skills, and proxemics, as shown in Figure 15.1. Kinesics is a sub-discipline of communication science and, as part of conversation analysis, specifically examines a person's behaviour and signals during negotiations (Stangl, 2022).

15.2.2 *Motor skills* (*the totality of all body movements*)

Motor skills encompass all movements and behaviour patterns of the body during negotiations. The term "motor skills" refers to the totality of all movement sequences of the human body. A distinction is made between gross and fine motor skills. Gross motor skills include movements involving the head, shoulders, torso, pelvis, arms, and legs (Schick, 2009). The movement of fingers, toes, and the face is part of the fine motor skills area.

15.2.3 Body language and gestures

Gestures are the totality of gestures that serve as movements in interpersonal communication. In particular, movements of the arms, hands, and head often accompany or replace messages in a given spoken language. Gestures, as signs of non-verbal communication, can be identified and decoded as signals during negotiations.

15.2.4 Facial expression and mimicry

Mimicry (or facial expressions) refers to the visible movements of the surface of the face. In most cases, an overall impression is created from individual facial facets since the individual movements of facial muscles occur within fractions of a second. Mimicry is a component of the expressive behaviour of humans as well as animals that are capable of it. In humans, it is an important part of non-verbal communication, along with other behaviours and actions such as gestures. Facial expressions primarily result from contractions of facial muscles and are produced in particular by the eyes and mouth, which are the most mobile parts of the face. There are approximately 3,000 variations.

15.2.5 Pantomime (expressive movements)

Pantomime is the totality of expressive movements, which include facial expressions, gestures, and body posture.

15.2.6 Taxis (head and torso signals)

In negotiations, taxis refers to non-verbal signals involving head or torso alignment. In this sense, taxis also includes eye contact.

15.2.7 Haptics (touch)

Haptics (tactile communication, or the sense of touch) describes touch as a component of non-verbal communication. There are four types of touch in non-verbal communication, as follows:

- self-touch,
- other-touch,

- object-tactile contact,
- imaginative touch.

Haptics is closely linked to the theory of proxemics (the study of spatial behaviour as part of body language). In both cases, we are dealing with personal space and territory. Touch is usually the direct result of letting others into our confidential zone. We obviously would not allow others to touch us if we did not feel comfortable being near them.

15.2.8 Locomotor skills (*movement behaviour*)

Locomotor skills, a sub-area of motor skills (ability to move and movement behaviour) refer to the following types of movement:

- movements causing a change in location (conscious and/or controlled) of the body, such as climbing, running, walking, and jumping;
- movements and (involuntary) reflexes of the body or parts of the body, for example, blushing or sweating when stressed;
- an individual's urge to move;
- experience of space (through the movements performed).

15.2.9 Proxemics (*distance behaviour*)

Proxemics examines and describes the signals that negotiators exchange by maintaining a certain distance from one another. Proxemics is an area of negotiation in psychology and communication sciences, as well as a sub-area of locomotor skills.

15.2.10 Paralanguage and prosody (*elements accompanying speech*)

Paralanguage refers to all vocal means that accompany speech, i.e., those linked to speech sounds, that are important for communication. The term paralanguage covers various phenomena of non-verbal communication, such as tone of voice, volume, filled ("uh…") or unfilled pauses, laughter, sighing, and the use or avoidance of dialect in spoken language. According to Paul Watzlawick's communication theory, paralanguage is the relational aspect of language. A discrepancy between the content aspect (digital signal) and the relational aspect (analogue signal) of speech is often perceived intuitively. Prosody refers to the totality of those phonetic properties of a language that are not linked to the sound or phoneme. These include word and sentence accents, intonation, sentence melody, tempo, rhythm, and pauses when speaking. In communication research, the vocal formation of words is observed in prosodics: Does the other person speak softly or harshly? When is the voice raised? Is it directed against something, or is the speaker emphasising his attentiveness? Is the voice combative, or does the speaker rely on a gentle, emotional conviction? Is the voice uncertain, or does it merely feign inner convictions? (Stangl, 2022).

15.2.11 *Eye contact and blinking*

Eye contact is the mutual gaze of a person with their eyes during negotiations. It is a dynamic, visual event. Eye contact is an important means of expressing body language and a central part of non-verbal communication. Especially in stressful situations where a person tries to remain calm and relaxed, the stress level is indicated by subconscious calming gestures, known as "adaptors". These small characteristics can show you, for example, whether a topic is particularly important to your counterpart, even though they may prefer not to reveal it. Frequent blinking may indicate uncertainty and deception. Likewise, an averted gaze can be a signal of disinterest.

15.2.12 *Physical environment* (*atmosphere of the negotiations*)

In addition to the content and organisational preparation (the right information, assessing the other side, choosing the strategy, setting the agenda, and seating arrangement), the environment and atmosphere are also important for a good outcome of the negotiation. The most fundamental decision is the choice of location. However, this choice also depends largely on the requirements of the negotiation. The first decision you have to make is a strategic one: Should the negotiation take place on "neutral" ground (a rented room) or in a room belonging to the other side? Or should the negotiations take place within your "own four walls"? Organisational considerations, too, must be taken into account. Are aids such as flip charts, a blackboard, or an overhead projector required? This also includes rental conditions (costs and duration) and organising overnight accommodations near the negotiation location. As a host, however, you should strive to take everything into your own hands: atmosphere, timing, and breaks. Also, consider the physical well-being of the participants: appropriate lighting, a comfortable room temperature, and, above all, enough water.

15.2.13 *Impression management*

Impression management (IM) is the conscious or unconscious control of the impression that people or organisations make on others. IM is increasingly being used as a concept in public relations. It can create or change images as an action concept. In German-language social psychology literature, the term "self-presentation" is also used synonymously.

15.2.14 *Chronemics (temporal signals of non-verbal communication)*

Chronemics, or chronicle, refers to the role of time in negotiations and non-verbal communication. In particular, chronemics involves the study of both subjective and objective human tempos when speaking, thinking, or considering, as these influence human behaviour and depend on it.

15.3 Decoding Signals Using the Three-Phase Model

15.3.1 *Decoding non-verbal communication signals*

The analysis of non-verbal communication is difficult because it involves people and behaviours (O'Brien, 2016). Micro expressions and expressions of non-verbal communication are often visible only for a few milliseconds (Helmold, 2022). When analysing non-verbal communication, attention should be paid to behavioural patterns and recurring cues. In this context, a baseline can be created from which behavioural patterns (clusters) may be identified through testing signals and stimuli, as shown in Figure 15.2. On this basis, recurring patterns in behaviour, facial expressions, and gestures can be discovered, allowing you to identify the meanings of various non-verbal signals (Thézé *et al.*, 2021). These insights and aids can then be used sensibly in your own negotiation strategy and tactics. The decoding

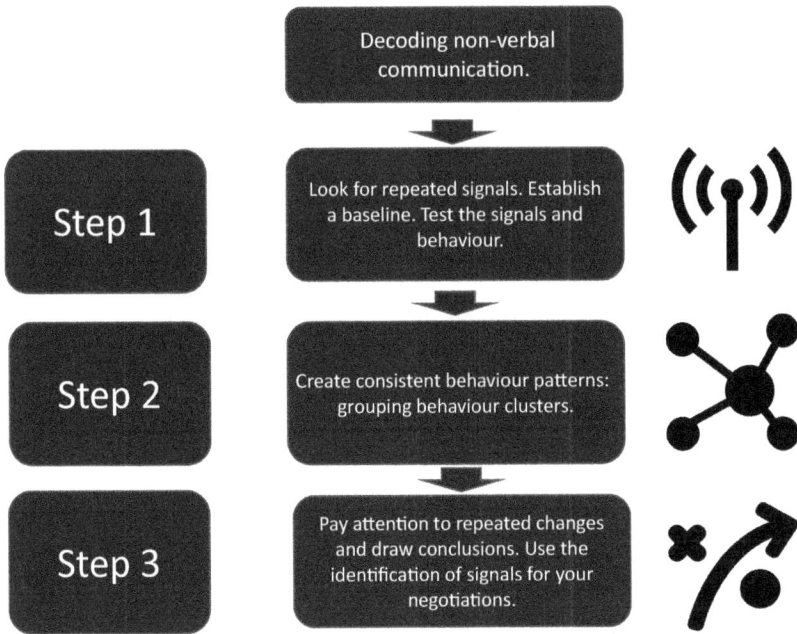

Figure 15.2. Decoding non-verbal signals.

of non-verbal signals also takes place in a variety of ways, consciously and unconsciously, based on knowledge or, with the help of mirror neurons, through empathic sympathy.

- The eye provides information about facial expressions, gestures, and body language, as well as movement patterns, proximity, and distance, vegetative symptoms (e.g., blushing, sweating, pupil size of the other person), and other aspects (see the section on eye contact).
- The receptors in the skin provide sensations that are assigned to the sense of touch, temperature, and pain. The sense of touch and tactile communication are based on sensations such as tickling, touch, vibration, pressure, and tension.
- The sense of smell (olfaction) determines, for example, whether you can "smell" another individual.
- In addition, the acoustic perception of the non-verbal components of speech, such as voice colour and pitch, as components of paraverbal communication, provides further information.

15.3.2 *Partially conscious non-verbal communication*

Certain body language signals are partially conscious. We usually note certain changes in our facial expressions ourselves, but for the most part, we do not perceive these changes nor can we consciously use them to communicate. Friedrich Nietzsche summed it up: One may lie with one's mouth, but with the mouth that one makes one still tells the truth. Certain autonomous body functions, such as sweating, blushing, pupil changes, or pulse, which are noticeable to the other person, cannot be consciously controlled but are partly perceptible (Loewenstein, 2021).

15.4   Facial Action Coding System: Decoding Facial Expressions

Paul Ekman and Wallace Friesen recognised the importance of facial expressions and micro expressions early on. In 1978, the two psychologists developed the so-called Facial Action Coding System (FACS), a method widely used by psychologists worldwide today to decode non-verbal signals. It gives us the ability to accurately recognise and decode the emotions of the other person based on the slightest of facial reactions. If you know the alphabet of facial expressions, it is easy to recognise quick signals.

15.5   Possible Signs of Untruths, Deception, or Exaggeration

In principle, neither side lies intentionally in negotiations or conflict discussions; instead, they conceal certain details or avoid addressing them, thereby strengthening their positions. For example, a buyer will not want to reveal to a seller that they have no alternative courses of action, even if they can only use products from this supplier. A salesperson, on the other hand, will not reveal that he will offer an order at cost, i.e., without making a profit (long-term price floor), in order to utilise existing capacity in his own factory, as otherwise production areas would be empty. Untruths, lies, or white lies are protective gestures that create stress, manifesting itself physically in various ways, as follows (Anston, 2019):

- pulling or scratching the earlobe,
- wringing the hands,

- licking the lips,
- wiping sweat from the forehead or neck,
- repeatedly tugging at clothing,
- unmotivated hair straightening,
- playing with the fingernails.

An inclined gaze, touching parts of the face, or a temporary deviation are signals of lying or exaggeration. Signals of untruths are difficult to detect; however, they can be uncovered through careful observation and by conducting in-depth, analytical negotiations. Exaggerations are particularly common in intercultural areas and are often viewed as lies by the recipient and negotiating partner. Touching the nose or earlobe, blinking, or shying away can be signs of untruths or exaggerations. In this situation, detailed questions should be asked, and analytical negotiation tools should be used to uncover exaggerations or lies. In principle, one should not assume a lie; instead, one should aim to uncover it through targeted counterquestions or identify exaggerations and build one's own strategy on that.

15.6 Signals of Stress

In negotiations, mistakes are quite often caused by stress. Under stress, the emotional side of people tends to become more prominent. Stress means tension, pressure, and physical signals such as a faster heartbeat, increased blood flow to the brain, muscular tension, or energy supply through blood sugar and fats. When stress occurs, the body is put under tension, and in dangerous situations, stimuli are passed on to the brain via the sensory organs: eyes, ears, or nose (Eckert and Tarnowski, 2022). Noradrenaline and adrenaline are released, putting the body into a state of maximum performance readiness. If the stress is successfully managed, the body returns to normal, and adrenaline breaks down. If the stress persists, however, the brain sends a request for more adrenaline. In this case, the second stress axis, known as the "wet" stress axis, is activated, leading to the release of cortisol into the bloodstream, thus enabling the body to adapt to the stressful situation while maintaining optimal performance levels. The increased release of cortisol signals danger to our system, and a chronic state of stress occurs. Over time, the adrenal glands can become exhausted and no longer produce enough cortisol. This means that the cortisol level drops below the normal level after the increase; symptoms include tiredness and a lack of energy (AOK, 2022). Science distinguishes between positive (eustress) and negative stress (distress). Distress is also referred to as negative stress (where "dis" is a Latin word).

Practical tip: Mirroring is a positive signal. People who get along well reflect each other's behaviour. If, for example, two men are sitting at a table in a restaurant, drinking beer, and mirror images of each other, you can immediately observe that they are having a good conversation. Or, for example, during a seminar break, when two participants are sitting in the hallway with their legs crossed and their arms folded, the individual gestures may signal rejection, but since the two are sitting in mirror images, the overall picture shows that they are getting on very well. In a conversation, you can mirror both body language and content. I follow my conversation partner in terms of content. If I have the feeling that he is comfortable in the conversation, then I will adjust my behaviour accordingly. If he follows me now, he feels comfortable, and we are in sync. This is also called the butterfly dance, or "we are on the same wavelength". My counterpart is now open to me. And only now do I begin to convey my content. We talk about this and that, and if I make changes, my counterpart will follow suit.

References

Anston, E. J. (2019). *Body Language: How to Analyze People, Use Powerful Communication, Manipulation and Negotiation Skills to Influence Anyone.* Amazon Digital Services LLC — KDP Print US.

AOK (2022). Strategien zur Stressbewältigung bei akutem und chronischem Stress. Available at: https://www.aok.de/pk/magazin/wohlbefinden/stress/stressbewaeltigung-tipps-fuer-akuten-und-chronischen-stress/.

Eckert, M. and Tarnowski, T. (2022). *Stress- und Emotionsregulation: Trainingsmanual zum Programm Stark im Stress.* Langensalza: Beltz Verlagsgruppe.

Helmold, M., Dathe, T., and Hummel, F. (2022). *Successful Negotiations. Best-in-Class Recommendations for Breakthrough Negotiations.* Cham: Springer.

Loewenstein, J. (2021). *Körpersprache — Menschen lesen: Wie Sie mit der Macht der nonverbalen Kommunikation Menschen für sich gewinnen, selbstbewusst Auftreten und die Psychologie anderer durchschauen.* Hamburg: Loewenstein.

O'Brien, J. (2016). *Negotiations for Procurement Professionals*, 2nd edn. Croyden: Kogan Page.

Raschl, J. (2021). *Körpersprache: Lerne wie die Körpersprache und die nonverbale Kommunikation der Menschen um dich herum zu analysieren und finde heraus was sie wirklich denken* (Psychologie für Anfänger). Independently published.

Schick, C. M. (2009). *Arbeitswissenschaft*, 3. Auflage. Berlin.

Stangl, W. (2022). Kinesik. *Online Lexikon für Psychologie und Pädagogik.*

Thézé, R., Giraud, A.-L., and Mégevand, P. (2021). The phase of cortical oscillations determines the perceptual fate of visual cues in naturalistic audiovisual speech. *Science Advances*, 6(45), eabc6348. Available at: https://doi.org/10.1126/sciadv.abc6348.

Chapter 16

Deblocking Negotiations

16.1 Reasons for Impasses and Deadlocks

Negotiations always reach impasses when the opponents see no tactical scope to move towards each other due to entrenched positions (which are usually based on inflexible insistence on their own point of view) because they believe that otherwise they will lose face (Unger, 2018). Impasses arise from differing (different) or contrary (opposing) interests and points of view of the negotiators, as shown in Figure 16.1. Such situations basically only allow two options:

- The path of least resistance in order not to let the negotiations collapse. One gives in in order not to jeopardise the conclusion of the negotiations. The conclusion as such, not the result itself, is the focus.
- Termination of the negotiations because no negotiation result is in sight. A conclusion can only be reached at the detriment of one's own side. The focus here is on the (bad) result itself, not on reaching a conclusion at any price.

Basically, a bad result always leaves at least one party dissatisfied. Therefore, breaking a deadlock should never lead to paying too much or accepting too little.

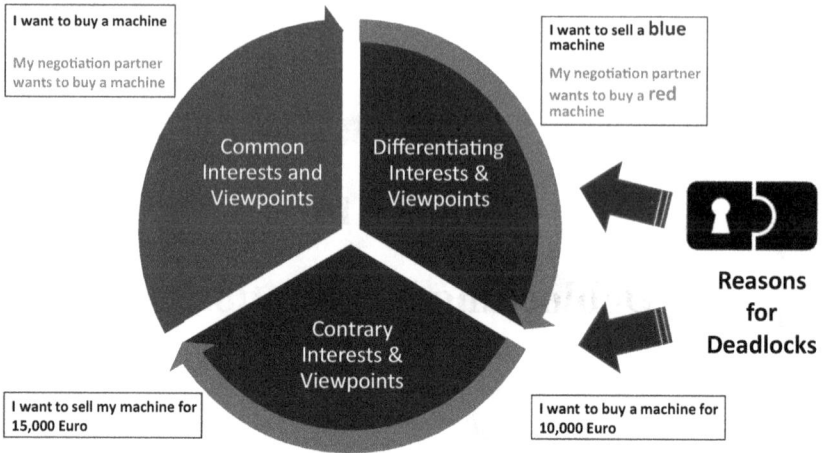

Figure 16.1.   Common, differentiating and contrary interests in negotiations.

16.2   Recommendations for Action to Get Out of a Deadlock

16.2.1 *Change the negotiation location*

In addition to the content and organisational preparation (e.g., the right information, assessing the other side, choosing the strategy, setting the agenda, and seating arrangement), the environment and atmosphere are also important for a good outcome of the negotiation. The most fundamental decision is the choice of location. You should be guided by the principle: Any place where you feel comfortable is suitable. The better you will be able to find and develop your self-confidence. As a host, however, you should pay attention to the right atmosphere, timing, and breaks. Also, consider the physical well-being of the participants: appropriate lighting, a comfortable room temperature, and, above all, enough water. In the case of deadlocks, you can change the negotiation location, for example, to a cultural event, a restaurant, or a bar. You can also show the negotiating opponents the sights in order to create a better atmosphere and break the ice.

16.2.2 *Giving in and making concessions*

All negotiations, however different they may be, have one thing in common: they always come to a point where concessions are expected and necessary. The main mistake here is that concessions are seen as weaknesses or failures. Behind this lies the (unfounded) fear that if you give in on one point, you will be forced to give in on other points as well. And that is precisely where the mistake lies. But the opposite is the case; basically, giving in means winning – if you are clear beforehand about how far and where you want (or can) to give in (Hoffmann, 2018). There are three ways to make concessions at one point in a negotiation:

- giving in without getting anything in return;
- giving in, not without value;
- giving in, but getting more.

The high art of giving in is making concessions on unimportant aspects of your own negotiation goals to which you receive something in return or additional value. Psychologically, you can see that the value of a concession is often measured by how hard you worked for it. A hard negotiation makes a concession more valuable than if it were granted in advance.

16.2.3 *Ask the how question*

Approach the negotiating partner and use a "how?" question to ask what options and solutions are there to get out of an impasse: "How can we do this?" or "How do you think this could work?" If the other side is interested in a deal, they will look for solutions.

16.2.4 *Issue warnings*

Speak directly to your negotiating partner and issue a warning. Warnings are often confused with threats. The key difference between a warning and a threat lies in its objectivity, wording, and tone of delivery. Warnings must be fact-based and should not be delivered emotionally. A warning could look like this: "I fear that, should we fail to clarify this point, our cooperation will become extremely difficult in the future. Do you intend to give up on the negotiation?"

16.2.5 *Focus on the essentials*

Another way to get out of an impasse is to concentrate on the essentials, leaving out the details. Most negotiations reach a dead end because of disputed details, even though both sides are largely in agreement. In this situation, let the principle of "let's get to it" guide you. Suggest to the other side that they set aside their existing problems for now, start working together, and "renegotiate" unresolved issues at a later date based on initial work results and experience. However, when using this approach, it is important to establish a clear written agreement that specifies all points, including those under dispute, with precision. Conditions or remuneration should only be negotiated and estimated for fixed agreements; as for disputed points, they form part of the renegotiation. Furthermore, it is essential to agree on a binding date for the renegotiation.

In many cases, it turns out that during the renegotiation, contentious points about the collaboration that had begun are resolved on their own. In cases where this is not the case, the parties part ways amicably, so to speak, because both sides have demonstrated their goodwill. However, it is important to keep detailed records of the trial phase in order to bring the renegotiation to a successful conclusion.

16.2.6 *Obtain more information by asking questions*

First, you should try to get as close as possible to the core of the problem by asking questions ("Is it too expensive?" or "What are you comparing it with?"; Michels, 2011). Once you have obtained more information, you can convince your negotiating partner by cleverly arguing, for example, by presenting the benefits of a product or common interests. If, contrary to expectations, no solution is found, it is better to break off negotiations rather than seeking a lazy compromise. A question can often be divided into several points (Dahms, 2022). In this case, you can leave the contentious issue aside for the time being and agree on partial results.

16.2.7 *Exchange negotiators*

Dead ends can have a variety of reasons. One reason that should not be underestimated is often the "chemistry" between the participants. A dispute over detailed questions is often just meant to conceal the fact that individual participants simply cannot stand each other, and a failure of the negotiation for such a "simple" reason is meant to be objectively examined in terms of the matter itself (Helmold, 2023).

The most sensible solution is to remove such a participant from the game if he is in your own negotiating team and bring in a new employee. This is of course not always easy, and in any case, you must prevent your colleague from taking it personally. This possible problem should also be clarified with the team during preparation. In addition, don't be afraid to remove yourself from the game if you find that there are irreconcilable differences with you. If you (and your team) are interested in a successful conclusion, then any means should be justified to achieve it. However, it should be obvious to you that even in cases where you suggest changes to your own negotiating team to the other side, you should insist on counter-performances that will help you achieve your negotiating goal.

16.2.8 *New player as a beacon of hope*

Dead ends often indicate that the initially positive and cooperative atmosphere in which the negotiation began has shifted to a highly competitive mode, hindering the progress of the negotiations. A change must be achieved here, and in order to bring about such a change, "a new player" who wants to work together rather than argue can be very helpful. If he has not yet appeared, then now is the time for your "good guy". Otherwise, your team should indeed consider bringing in a "new player" to the game. You could, for example, call such a "player" a speaker or reporter. If the negotiation reaches a dead end because the other side is sceptical of your statements (for example, your descriptions of the product or service you want to sell), it can help to bring in a practitioner who has the experience and credibility to make your claims believable.

16.2.9 *Tell a joke*

Whenever negotiations reach a dead end, tensions arise in communication that also stand in the way of a solution. Believe it or not, a well-told joke is often just the right way to resolve tensions and continue negotiations in a relaxed atmosphere (Unger, 2018). However, it requires a fair amount of impudence. For example, in the early 1970s, influential individuals at Ford headquarters came to the conclusion that the Mercury Cougar should be taken off the market. Henry Ford II called a conference, which was also attended by the head of the Lincoln-Mercury division. He was of the opinion that such a decision was grotesque because a puma ("cougar") was Mercury's advertising symbol and slogan ("The sign of the cat"). There was rare unanimity at the meeting. When Ford II finally asked the Lincoln-Mercury manager for his opinion, he replied: "I can only say one thing: you can't run a cat household without a cat". It is said that it was this joke that saved the life of the Mercury Cougar.

16.2.10 *Make an ultimatum calmly but firmly*

An ultimatum is a diplomatic request – often for a limited period – to resolve a pending matter satisfactorily under the threat of harsh counter-measures if the other party does not comply. An ultimatum can be made; however, it carries a 50:50 chance of agreement. An ultimatum should only be issued if there is evidence that the other side is interested in a solution (Helmold *et al.*, 2022).

16.2.11 *Expanding the scope of negotiations*

Negotiations that are in a deadlock can be successful by expanding the scope and adding more scope.

16.2.12 *Postponing negotiations*

The very last resort when negotiations reach a deadlock and all attempts to counteract it have been unsuccessful is to request a postponement of the negotiations.

Practical tip: Try to unblock the deadlock and get out of the deadlock by introducing new, fresh players.

References

Dahms, C. (2022). Emotionale Intelligenz – *Empathisch & erfolgreich durchs Leben: Wie Sie Ihre Beziehungen nachhaltig verbessern, zielführend kommunizieren und sich ein positives Umfeld aufbauen.* Hamburg: Loewenstein.

Hoffmann, T. (2018). *Das FBI-Prinzip: Verhandlungstaktiken für Gewinner.* München: Ariston.

Helmold, M. (2023). *Verhandlungen gewinnen. Konzepte, Methoden und Tools.* Cham: Springer.

Helmold, M., Dathe, T., and Hummel, F. (2022). *Successful Negotiations: Best-in-Class Recommendations for Breakthrough Negotiations.* Wiesbaden: Springer.

Michels, G. (2011). Erfolgreich verhandeln (II). Wege aus der Sackgasse. Available at: https://www.pharmazeutische-zeitung.de/ausgabe-452011/wege-aus-der-sackgasse/ [Abgerufen am 12 July 2022].

Unger, A. (2018). Drohendes Scheitern. Die beste Strategie, wenn Verhandlungen in eine Sackgasse geraten. Available at: https://www.impulse.de/management/unternehmensfuehrung/verhandlungen-drohendes-scheitern/7299608.html [Abgerufen am 12 July 2022].

Chapter 17

Power and Power Balance in Negotiations

17.1 Power: Subject and Definition

Power is an element in every communication and negotiation process (Schumann *et al.*, 2023). For negotiators, it is therefore important to consider power elements and conflict situations in negotiations (Pfetsch, 2006). "Bargaining power", a term used in various negotiation theories, comprises negotiation and power and describes the relative strength of the negotiating positions between people or organisations during the balance of interests. Bargaining power is generally used to describe dominance in a negotiation over the other side. Bargaining power is instrumentalised in negotiations in order to reach an agreement (such as the distribution of monetary values). The instrument of bargaining power is the ability to influence the other party in one's own favour in order to achieve an increase in profits. The relative strength of bargaining power is measured by its specific relationship to the party involved. It is greater when one side can enforce its own demands in a negotiation. If the negotiating power between the parties is equal, there is a balanced result. According to this classification, bargaining power can ultimately be quantified as a unit of measurement (ratio), enabling it to describe the relative advantages or strengths.

17.2 Showing Power through Competence

Formal and informal power are important elements in negotiations and transactions. The formally specified position-based power is based mainly on hierarchical structures and hierarchy levels, which are usually shown in an organisational chart, while informal power is not necessarily based on this basis. The formal organisational structure is the result of a structured and systematic hierarchy that management considers appropriate. The basic elements of the organisational structure are positions that are categorised into groups and departments as subsystems, as well as the reporting channels. The cooperation between the subsystems is determined by the process organisation that regulates the work processes. The organisational chart is a graphic representation of the organisational structure that shows communication channels and processes. In addition to formal power, there are also power structures that are not immediately visible and are based on informal circumstances. Often, people are granted special authority by the members of a group because of their personal characteristics (e.g., high level of technical competence, long-term collaboration, and extensive experience). An informal leader can have an integrating and stabilising effect. However, conflicts can also arise with the superior (the formal leader).

17.3   Formal Power

Formal power refers to the ability of a person or group in the hierarchy of a company or organisation to make decisions within a defined scope through their function and to negotiate them. Managers possess formal power by virtue of their employment contract.

17.4   Informal Power

However, in business and negotiation practices, it is often found that the officially defined structure is usually not identical to the actual structure. In addition to the formal company organisation, informal or informal phenomena arise as a result of unplanned human behaviour. The reason for this is the individual needs and ideas of the employees. They appear in the following informal forms:

• interest groups,
• communication,
• processes,

- organisational structures,
- norms,
- leaders.

If the formal and informal power structures are understood, they form the starting point for recognising and overcoming resistance. Formal power structures consist of the organisational structure and the process organisation. Informal power structures are more likely to arise from charismatic leaders and their experience, knowledge, or membership in a group. Informal leaders can be identified by the undercover agent or informant and be used for the negotiation success. Informal leaders may have their own individual goals and interests. It is important to consider this and to help that the informal leaders achieve their goals (Helmold *et al.*, 2022). If the organisational structure and process organisation are known, negotiation success can be achieved through either positive or negative negotiations. If warnings from the other side are not taken seriously, the warning should always be put into action.

17.5 Agile Negotiation in the VUCA World

Digitalisation, demographic change, and globalisation – our world is changing. It is changing in many places simultaneously, often unexpectedly, with no sign of an end to this permanent shift (Helmold, 2023). The acronym "VUCA" describes the challenges that our constantly changing world presents to companies. It stands for the following:

- Volatility/Changeability
- Uncertainty
- Complexity
- Ambiguity

However, in order to cope with unknown, changing challenges, we need the ability to adapt our strategies, structures, and processes to the actual circumstances in the short term. Keeping dynamics and stability in a changing environment in such a balance that the business mission can be fulfilled in the long term requires a new way of thinking and working at all levels of the company. In our understanding, this process is appropriately described by the term "agility". Agility in negotiations is the dexterity, agility, or mobility of negotiation teams and individuals within lean and flat structures and processes. You react flexibly to unforeseen events and new requirements. You are not only reactive but also proactive, for example, with regard to changes.

17.6 Power Games and Manipulation

Power games in negotiations are interactions between opponents who want to prove to each other that they possess more power than their counterparts. Power games are aimed at manipulation. In comparison to a negotiation strategy, a manipulative negotiation tactic is a manoeuvre that is used consciously: a move, countermove, or adjustment that is used to achieve the best possible result at a given time. Power games can also be used manipulatively by another party to move you from a safe position to a defensive position in which you are more vulnerable. As a negotiator, you must be prepared for such tactics at every opportunity. Power games can be ended in the following ways:

- Thorough preparation: If you prepare thoroughly for the power games, you don't have to bend yourself internally. You can work with different types of players and achieve something, regardless of level or position, whether you are a managing director in a medium-sized company or a corporate board member.
- Awareness of the role in the game of power: If you are clearly aware of your negotiating position and role, you are less susceptible to power games. The better you know yourself and the more honestly you perceive yourself, your actions, and your words, the easier it is to make and defend decisions.
- See through your negotiating opponent; end power games: If you pay careful attention not only to the words but also to the behaviour of your counterpart, you are more likely to see through power games. If what is said and what they do don't match, the other player may not be as trustworthy as they initially assured you. A healthy gut feeling helps you to make decisions despite doubts, stay true to yourself, and achieve your goals.

Practical tip: Show power and conduct the negotiations from the driver's seat. If your negotiating partner perceives you as powerless, he may not take you seriously and want to use this to his advantage. Therefore, do not let your negotiating partner believe that he can manage the negotiation alone. If this is the case, you should take action and make it clear to the other person emphatically but firmly that there will be no one-sided solution.

References

Helmold, M. (2023). *Verhandlungen gewinnen. Konzepte, Methoden und Tools.* Cham: Springer.

Helmold, M., Dathe, T., and Hummel, F. (2022). *Successful Negotiations: Best-in-Class Recommendations for Breakthrough Negotiations.* Wiesbaden: Springer.

Pfetsch, F. R. (2006). *Verhandeln in Konflikten: Grundlagen – Theorie – Praxis* (German edition). Wiesbaden: VS Verlag für Sozialwissenschaften.

Schumann, R., *et al.* (2023). *System of Negotiations. Game Theory and Behavioral Economics in Procurement – the Guide for Professionals.* Cham: Springer.

Chapter 18

Negotiations of Claims

18.1 Claim Management: Subject and Definition

Claim management, or complaint management, in business relationships refers to the management of claims or demands that arise after the conclusion of a contract due to service disruptions. Service disruptions are properties or performance characteristics of a product that were contractually agreed upon by both the customer and supplier but not delivered. In German legal terms, this is referred to as a "material defect". Material defects typically result from poor design, defective manufacturing, or defective materials. In addition to material defects, other service disruptions include early or late deliveries, deliveries to undisclosed locations, or missing functions. In companies, performance disruptions are often referred to as non-conformities (Vidogah and Ndegukuri, 1988). In this context, supplementary claim management, or addendum management, plays a central role in negotiating these missing properties. Supplementary claim management is also called claim management or regression. Supplementary claims are usually made by the customer (the purchasing company) after the service has been provided and delivered due to deficits in quality, quantity, time, or type of delivery (customer supplementary claims), unless specified and agreed in contracts. Supplementary claims can also be made by the supplier (the delivering company) (i.e., supplier supplementary claims). Claim management is a discipline that has so far received limited attention in both research and teaching (Helmold, 2013).

In supplier management, supplementary claim management aims to amicably clarify the consequences of events during the course of the project that were not foreseeable when the contract was concluded. After the client places an order with the contractor, changes, additions, or extensions usually occur, particularly in large projects. Possible reasons are usually delivery failures, delays, or quality deviations. In their study, Hendricks and Singhal found that disruptions in the supply chain can reduce the company's value by up to 40% (Hendricks and Singhal, 2005), so the primary goal of claim management is prevention, as stated by numerous authors (Wieland and Wallenburg, 2012). Delivery failures due to force majeure, such as floods or earthquakes, are also covered. In cases of force majeure, additional claims may also be legally feasible under certain conditions. In particular, claims for damages can be made in the event of deficiencies in security and prevention, for example, in cases of gross negligence. Changes or extensions covered by the order do not lead to additional claims. If this is not the case, the contractor can make a subsequent claim for the additional costs incurred to the person responsible for the change or extension. Examples of this include the following:

- lost profits due to production downtime,
- costs for remedying defects and repairs,
- costs incurred in connection with troubleshooting (including shunting costs),
- compensation for damages due to a service failure,
- late or early delivery,
- storage costs for deliveries that are too early,
- transport costs for returning the goods for repair,
- packaging costs for new packaging,
- administrative costs for processing the subsequent claim.

18.2 Active and Passive Claim Management

18.2.1 *Active claim management*

Active claim management involves preparing and conducting negotiations with clients and contractors to determine whether claims can be asserted. This begins with a detailed analysis of the existing contract. This includes, for example, the following questions: How is the scope of services defined, and which formalities must be observed? The contract forms the legal basis for possible claims that can be asserted.

18.2.2 *Passive claim management*

With passive claim management, one's own claims are not enforced; however, all of the contractual partner's demands are accepted in order to avoid conflicts and prevent the termination of the business relationship. To avoid this from happening, it is advisable to carry out claim management before the contract is concluded. The following steps can help you anticipate additional costs and regulate potential claims contractually.

18.3 Phases in Supplementary Claim Management

In the event of service disruptions, the phase model shown in Figure 18.1 can be used, which suggests a structured, systematic approach to supplementary claims. If service features are not provided, and this is announced by purchasing or sales, supplementary claims can be asserted as follows. In phase 1, the supplementary claim manager is involved and consulted. In phase 2, he checks the extent to which service features deviate from the purchase contract through discussions with the functions involved, such as purchasing, sales, development, and quality management. He also documents the facts. In addition to elements such as the purchase contract, specification, service description, date of occurrence of the event, evidence

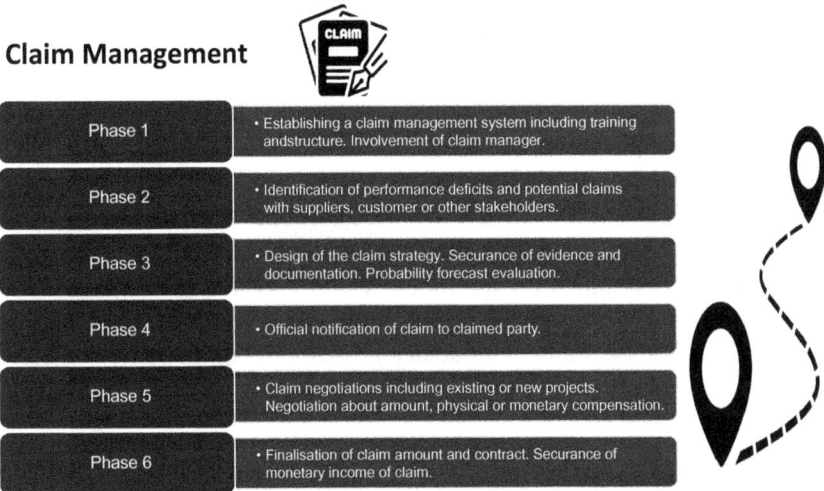

Claim Management

Phase 1	• Establishing a claim management system including training and structure. Involvement of claim manager.
Phase 2	• Identification of performance deficits and potential claims with suppliers, customer or other stakeholders.
Phase 3	• Design of the claim strategy. Securance of evidence and documentation. Probability forecast evaluation.
Phase 4	• Official notification of claim to claimed party.
Phase 5	• Claim negotiations including existing or new projects. Negotiation about amount, physical or monetary compensation.
Phase 6	• Finalisation of claim amount and contract. Securance of monetary income of claim.

Figure 18.1. Claim management.

of deviations, description, and justification, the documentation includes the assessment of the supplementary claim and the probability of a successful supplementary claim from a legal perspective (Helmold, 2013). Invoices, witness statements, photographs, correspondence, or expert opinions may serve as evidence here. Modern companies maintain a centralised, electronic record of additional expenses in a separate cost centre, whereas conventional organisations choose the paper route. Phase 3 then deals with the strategy for the additional claim. Managers often want compensation for all expenses and therefore make claims for damages for all associated costs, such as production downtime, rework, and administration work related to the additional claims. In the event of production downtime on production lines, it can lead to expenses running into the millions and push suppliers towards financial ruin; therefore, a strategy is required (MIK, 2017). Additional claims can be made in different ways, as follows:

• replacement deliveries after the additional claim has been asserted;
• conversion of the purchase contract and reimbursement of the purchase price;
• claims for damages for all costs of a replacement purchase;
• claims for damages for all direct costs, such as new purchases or repairs;
• claims for damages for all associated costs, such as production downtime, rework, and administration work related to the additional claims;
• offsetting an additional claim against future orders;
• offsetting an additional claim against existing orders.

Phase 4 begins the assertion of the additional claim to either the customer or the supplier with the transmission of the additional claim and a deadline to respond to it. It is important to take deadlines and hierarchical levels into account here to ensure that the additional claim is legally valid. Phase 4 is therefore a step that requires legal expertise. Phase 5 involves the actual negotiation of the additional claim with the other party. After successful negotiations, phase 6 must then ensure that the agreement is ratified. Ratification leads to monetary or material compensation.

18.4 Recommendations for Claim Management

Claim management is a central negotiation point for many companies in their business transactions. Claims must therefore be negotiated professionally, either actively or passively. It is therefore advisable not to involve lawyers in negotiations of claims, as this would negatively affect the relationship management between customers and suppliers. The use of lawyers is expensive; therefore, this step should be carefully considered. Claims always aim to improve performance, not primarily to achieve savings. Companies should employ contract managers who are actively involved in claim management. A position worth EUR 70,000–80,000 per year is likely to pay for itself within a short period of time. Companies should pursue their claims with foresight as part of their strategy. An example is waiving a claim in order to achieve cost reductions and savings in the next project (Helmold, 2023). In this context, other concessions are also negotiable, e.g., the provision of service staff or free replacement. Claims are used as a strategic tool in negotiations, and they should therefore be well documented to ensure sufficient evidence and materials are available during the negotiations. Claims and negotiations must not put a strain on the business relationship (Helmold and Terry, 2016). Finally, it is recommended that claims and claim values be realistically evaluated and analysed in a reasonable proportion to the actual damage. Table 18.1 summarises the recommendations for innovative claim management.

Table 18.1. Claim recommendation.

Claims or additional demands always aim to improve performance, not primarily to achieve savings.

Companies should employ claim managers who work in additional demand management. A position worth EUR 80,000 per year will probably pay for itself within a short period of time.

Companies should pursue their claims with foresight in their strategy. Example: waiving a claim in order to achieve cost reductions and savings in the next project.

Additional demands are used as a strategic tool in negotiations.

Additional demands and negotiations must not put a strain on business relationships.

Claims should be evaluated and analysed realistically in relation to the actual damage.

Lawyers, especially external lawyers, should stay in the background and not intervene in the negotiations.

References

Helmold, M. (2013). Claim-Management in der Praxis. Was tun bei Leistungsstörungen in der Lieferkette. *FM-Logistik*, 1-2/2013, 76–77.

Helmold, M. (2023). *Verhandlungen gewinnen. Konzepte, Methoden und Tools.* Cham: Springer.

Helmold, M. and Terry, B. (2016). *Lieferantenmanagement 2030.* Wiesbaden: Springer Gabler.

Hendricks, K. B., and Singhal, V. R. (2005). An empirical analysis of the effect of supply chain disruptions on long-run stock price performance and equity risk of the firm. *Production Operations Management*, 21(5), 501–522.

MIK (2017). Lieferausfälle BMW und Bosch verhandeln über Schadensersatz. Available at: http://www.spiegel.de/wirtschaft/unternehmen/bmw-und-bosch-verhandeln-ueber-schadensersatz-wegen-lieferausfaellen-a-1156486.html [Accessed on 26 May 2017].

Vidogah, W. and Ndegukuri, I. (1998). Improving the management of claims on construction contracts: Consultant's perspective. *Construction Management and Economics*, 16(3), 363–372.

Wieland, A. and Wallenburg, C. M. (2012). Dealing with supply chain risks: Linking risk management practices and strategies to performance. *International Journal of Physical Distribution & Logistics Management*, 42(10), 887–905.

Chapter 19

Warning Signals and Executing Warnings

19.1 Warning Signs as a Suitable Method in Negotiations

According to negotiation experts, warnings occur in the mind of the nego-tiating opponent, indicating potential consequences for failing on indi-vidual points or throughout the entire negotiation process (Schranner, 2015). If no agreement is reached, the other side might imagine a horrify-ing scenario of what could occur, such as by asking: "What will happen if we don't agree?" If you think that the negotiating partner is not aware of the strength of your own position, you can ask them, "What do you think I will do if we can't agree now?" The questions must be asked "openly". The more openly the question is formulated, the more information the negotiation partner needs to provide. However, it is important that the desire for a common solution be emphasised simultaneously (Helmold *et al*., 2022). Another variant in such a situation is the question, "What should I do according to your advice?" Here, the negotiating partner is also recognised in his position because he is asked for advice, signalling that his expertise and knowledge are trusted. At the same time, this is the ideal way to start a smooth conversation because his thoughts are "run-ning" again. But what do you do if the warning is ignored? Because it may be that the other person does not believe the warning. Therefore, the cred-ibility of a warning should always be shown to him visually. In this way, you demonstrate what you are planning without actually doing it.

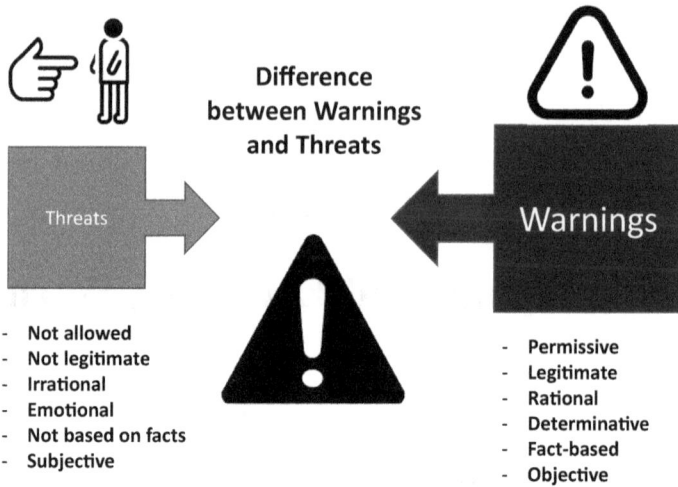

Difference between Warnings and Threats

Threats

Warnings

- Not allowed
- Not legitimate
- Irrational
- Emotional
- Not based on facts
- Subjective

- Permissive
- Legitimate
- Rational
- Determinative
- Fact-based
- Objective

Figure 19.1.   Warning and threats.

19.2 Warnings and Threats

In contrast to threats, warnings are allowed in negotiations. Warnings are based on facts and represent a clear message to the negotiating partner that the negotiations could fail. They represent the rational prediction of a possible upcoming termination of negotiations, which can still be prevented or mitigated. It draws attention to an impending danger. Figure 19.1 shows the major differences between warnings and threats.

19.3 Implement Warnings

If the negotiating partner still refuses to give in after a warning, then it becomes crucial to act and implement the warning. The other party must understand unequivocally that they cannot win unilaterally and that it is actually in their interest to return to the negotiating table (Kellner, 2000). The goal, therefore, is again a satisfactory agreement. Such means should only be used until one's own goals are achieved, not merely to win. Because every action leads to a reaction. The more aggressive your own methods are, the more bitterly your negotiation partner reacts. As a result, the very resistance that should actually be overcome hardens. In this situation, too, the following applies: the negotiating partner should not be cornered. A cornered opponent is dangerous. He will act rashly and irrationally. He should always be given a way out – a bridge that he can cross. It shows professionalism in building him a "golden bridge". And if the negotiating partner does not cross the bridge offered? Then, it is time to make the warning come true and implement all the announced actions (Helmold, 2023). Anyone who backs out now will lose face and make themselves look ridiculous and untrustworthy.

Practical tip: Use and implement warnings; make this clear to your negotiation opponent.

Practical tip: How to react to threats?

- First, it's crucial to identify threatening tactics.
- Ultimatums: "If you don't agree to X, we're walking away".
- Pressure Plays: "Your competitor would be happy to accept these terms".
- Emotional Manipulation: "This deal is too important to fall through!"
- Reacting impulsively to threats can be detrimental.
- Do Nothing: Silence can be powerful. Maintain eye contact and project confidence.
- Call It Out: "I sense you're trying to pressure me. Let's focus on finding a mutually beneficial solution".
- Pause or Delay: "This is a significant decision. May we reconvene after some time to reflect?"

References

Helmold, M. (2023). *Verhandlungen gewinnen. Konzepte, Methoden und Tools.* Cham: Springer.

Helmold, M., Dathe, T., and Hummel, F. (2022). *Successful Negotiations: Best-in-Class Recommendations for Breakthrough Negotiations.* Wiesbaden: Springer.

Kellner, H. (2000). *Rhetorik. Hart verhandeln – erfolgreich argumentieren.* München/Wien: Hanserverlag.

Schranner, M. (2015). 7 Prinzipien für erfolgreiches Verhandeln. [Abgerufen am 20 March 2018].

Chapter 20

New Approaches in Negotiations Using Neurolinguistic Programming

20.1 Neurolinguistic Programming (NLP) as a Negotiation Tool

20.1.1 *NLP technique: Subject and definition*

Neurolinguistic programming (NLP) views itself as a toolbox for communication, leadership, and negotiations. NLP emerged from the approach of analysing the behaviour of particularly successful people, aiming to derive action measures and leadership approaches (Holzfuss and Frank-Hollzfuss, 2020). NLP describes the essential processes by which people perceive themselves and their environments, process that information, feel and act on this basis, and communicate, learn, and change in relation to one another.

Figure 20.1 shows the process of NLP systematics employing a neuro approach to understanding how information is processed and passed on. Through language (linguistics), the information is conveyed in such a way that changes can be brought about (programming).

20.1.2 *Possible uses of the NLP technique*

NLP can be used in many ways in life, such as to change undesirable behaviour, improve one's own verbal and non-verbal communication, create understanding and be understood, support educational issues, and

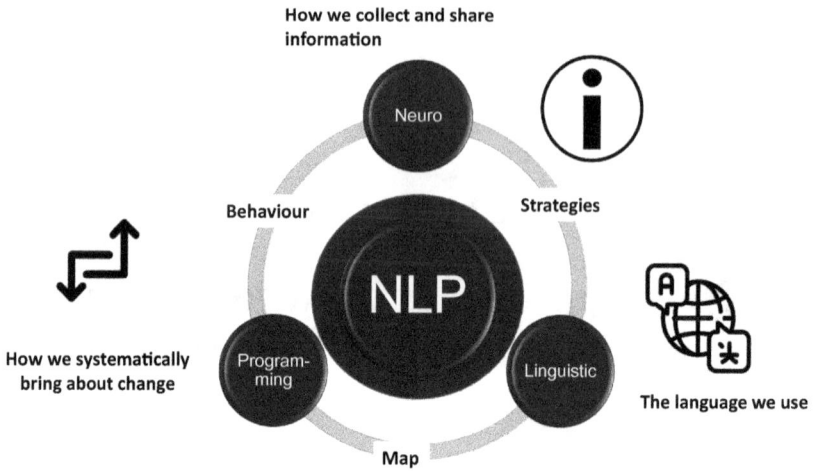

Figure 20.1. NLP in negotiations.

intensify both personal and professional relationships (Kuehl, 2020). NLP offers highly effective methods and techniques to individually assess one's negotiation style and the position. NLP approaches negotiation from a different perspective. Instead of focusing on the position of each negotiation side, it approaches it from the structural point of view. Each position of the two negotiation parties, even if radically opposed to the other, has a positive intent (Buchner, 1994). NLP provides the negotiator with not only strategies for dealing with individual stakeholders but also techniques for team-building and personal development. Through individual coaching, the manager learns to reflect on his or her own behaviour during daily work and to implement appropriate behaviour in accordance with the respective goals. NLP for managers includes the following:

- assessing people correctly (body language, facial expressions, and eyes),
- questioning facts,
- quickly identifying problems,
- conflict resolution strategies,
- recognising people's needs,
- understanding different worldviews,
- understanding roles and using them correctly,

- understanding situations with 1-2-3 perception positions,
- quick-wittedness techniques,
- state management (dealing with myself),
- understanding projects as a system.

20.2 Use of Artificial Intelligence (AI) in Negotiations

20.2.1 *AI as negotiation support through the use of digital apps*

AI can take on various tasks in negotiations, thereby reducing the time and effort required by human negotiators. Today, there is a growing number of negotiation support systems and automated negotiation agents that can support human negotiators before and during the process. They can serve as simulators and training tools; however, they also conduct negotiations to a certain extent autonomously (Dobrijević and Đoković, 2020).

Negotiation is a fundamentally human act between two or more individuals. When it comes to supplier negotiations, it is determined by the prior (and future) relationship between human counterparties. While digital processes can support this mission, if a key decision-maker involved in a supplier negotiation goes on vacation, changes jobs, or is hit by a bus(!), the negotiation will stall or struggle to close. It is a good reminder that, no matter what role AI plays in a negotiation, the negotiation process and award decision are driven by humans. The real purpose of AI is to make human negotiators more effective by reducing their time spent on busy work (rather than removing them from the negotiation process). This insight into how technology can augment and empower procurement teams (rather than replacing them) is fundamental. For those participating in vendor negotiations, it's likely that their companies book travel through a digital app that aggregates and discounts airline tickets. It's also likely that the hotel and transportation to the meeting are booked through digital apps. Therefore, the technology stack that supports this "face-to-face meeting" is mediated by a variety of digital apps (many of which already leverage AI), apps that support (rather than displace) the crucial face-to-face business negotiation by reducing the number of low-value transactional tasks and phone calls.

Given that digital apps are transforming the business processes of every other corporate department, it's unlikely that procurement negotiators will remain the sole exception to this trend. Applying AI to market and vendor data analysis doesn't mean that face-to-face negotiations will end; rather, it means they will be different – hopefully faster, better, and with fewer email chains and constantly changing spreadsheets.

20.2.2 *AI as negotiation support with algorithms*

Negotiations are carried out interactively between two or more parties. Negotiations are mostly carried out by people. However, algorithms and AI can also be used for rational decisions. There are certainly many rational decisions that have to be made in purchasing. This is where algorithms can show their strengths. Negotiation algorithms are applicable procedural rules, leading to solutions of certain problems within a finite number of steps. In such situations, algorithms can select the most suitable option for your own company. More and more large corporations are therefore delegating the responsibility of disseminating information to AI.

20.2.3 *AI as negotiation support with big data*

As big data reveal the purchasing behaviour of customers and clients, procurement professionals can understand user and supplier behaviours and plan negotiation strategies and media accordingly. However, success depends on the availability of virtual inventory in real time that evolves through self-learning to anticipate and meet this demand and reinvents the customer experience.

The future negotiator will not only be able to conduct an informed, reactive negotiation using AI-powered insights but will also be able to predict demand and negotiate proactively and have the product or service catalogue ready for use by the business user. The system will also be able to record, cognitively understand, and draw patterns from past negotiations to provide suggestive tactics or strategies.

20.2.4 *Use of chatbots*

All advances in AI will most likely result in a "have" and "have not" situation between those who possess AI capabilities and those who don't when it comes to effective negotiation. Now, let's imagine a scenario that is highly anticipated and could become a reality in the near future: negotiations conducted by an AI chatbot. The big question is, can a chatbot without common sense and emotions conduct negotiations like humans?

The answer lies in the advancements in the natural language processing branch of AI. Natural language processing is the next big thing in AI, and it is only a matter of time before we can interact with machines daily, not only for personal use (e.g., Google Home, Amazon Alexa, Microsoft Cortana) but also for business purposes. Once conversational user interfaces slowly replace traditional graphical user interfaces and then are equipped with all the data, machine learning, and language skills, a negotiating chatbot will not be too distant or difficult to visualise. The biggest challenge will be that, as humans, we tend to forget we can approach things in a new way. However, at the same time, we are also able to adapt to changes quickly. In other words, technology could completely and irreversibly change the way procurement negotiates in the very near future. It will definitely be a very exciting journey. Are we on board yet?

References

Buchner, D. (1994). *NLP im Business: Konzepte für Veränderungscoaching.* Wiesbaden: Springer.

Dobrijević, D. and Đoković, F. (2020). E-Negotiation: Can Artificial Intelligence Negotiate Better Deals? Available at: https://portal.sinteza.singidunum.ac.rs/paper/760 [Abgerufen am 15 July 2022].

Holzfuss, B. and Frank-Hollzfuss, J. (2020). *Das NLP Practitioner Prüfungswissen kompakt: Die Wissensessenz aus zehn Jahren erfolgreicher NLP Ausbildung.* Unabhängig publiziert.

Kuehl, A. L. (2020). *NLP für Anfänger – Das richtige Mindset für Ihre Persönlichkeitsentwicklung: Wie Sie Ihre Gedanken kontrollieren und das eigene Unterbewusstsein programmieren um erfolgreicher im Leben zu werden.*

Index

www.ingramcontent.com/pod-product-compliance
Lightning Source LLC
Chambersburg PA
CBHW061250220326
41599CB00028B/5603